THE

1%

DIFFERENCE

Small Change-Big Impact

Murray Lyons and Kelly Lyons

Bloomington, IN

authorHOUSE®
Milton Keynes, UK

AuthorHouse™
1663 Liberty Drive, Suite 200
Bloomington, IN 47403
www.authorhouse.com
Phone: 1-800-839-8640

AuthorHouse™ UK Ltd.
500 Avebury Boulevard
Central Milton Keynes, MK9 2BE
www.authorhouse.co.uk
Phone: 08001974150

First published by AuthorHouse 10/2/2006

ISBN: 1-4259-5651-3 (sc)

*Printed in the United States of America
Bloomington, Indiana*

This book is printed on acid-free paper.

CONTENTS

INTRODUCTION 1

CHAPTER ONE...5

CHAPTER TWO...13

CHAPTER THREE...23

CHAPTER FOUR 45

CHAPTER FIVE 57

CHAPTER SIX 71

CHAPTER SEVEN 83

CHAPTER EIGHT 101

CHAPTER NINE...115

CHAPTER TEN 129

CHAPTER ELEVEN 135

EPILOGUE..139

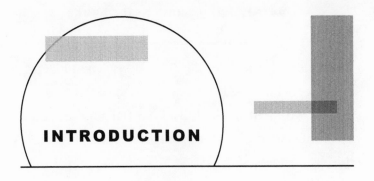

INTRODUCTION

Business is about creating value and generating profit. If you know how to do this, you become more valuable, not only to your present employer but also to future employers. The bottom line is that employees who create value are valued.

Every day employees make decisions that ultimately get reflected in the financials. In many businesses, sales reps exert the most impact on the financial success of a business because their decisions directly affect the most important line on the income statement—the sales line—however; other employee groups can significantly influence financial results. Purchasing affects costs of goods sold; managers, supervisors and employees affect expenses; other employees affect the utilization of assets such as inventory, receivables and fixed assets; and *everyone* affects productivity.

In order to understand the economic value you create, you must first have a basic understanding of how your decisions are reflected in the financials and the multiplier affect of those decisions. The universal language of business is money, so it is to your advantage to have strong business skills, financial acumen and a clear understanding of the profit drivers and profit leaks in your business.

You may be saying to yourself, *I'm just one person; what difference can I possibly make?* or *One percent doesn't make a much of a difference, so why bother?* Most of us believe senior managers and special teams make the decisions that really make a difference and to a certain extent they do. Furthermore, concepts like re-engineering have taught us to go for the home run and be less concerned about smaller day-to-day decisions. A natural outcome is to believe that the decisions we make everyday are insignificant in the overall picture.

The good news for people in business is that a mere 1 percent improvement in key variables they influences every day can have a huge impact on profitability in a very short period of time. You do not have to make significant investments or wait years for the result. You do not have to create teams and initiate projects nor do you have to add any work to your current workload. You can make a difference today and start to see the results by month end!

So why don't we hear more about this amazing principle? Because, again, we have been conditioned to believe that 1 percent is too miniscule to matter and that hitting a home run requires a new product, new markets and new technology, which, of course, is someone else's responsibility . . . but nothing could be further from the truth!

In most organizations, a mere 1 percent improvement in the choices employees make every day can improve net profitability by 20%-100%! Even better is that most employees are easily able to make a 1 percent improvement—after all, this is not a "stretch" goal.

Why is it important for your employer to be profitable? Why should you focus on helping the business to make more money? These are legitimate questions, which we answer in the following way:

1. Profitable companies offer more security, something we all crave;
2. Growing and profitable businesses create opportunities you might be interested in;
3. Employees who know how to create positive financial results become more valuable to both current and future employers (that's a good thing for you!);
4. Companies always need people with strong business skills and financial acumen. These

skills are in short supply and therefore can be a competitive advantage for both you and your employer;

5. If you manage, run or own a business, these skills are invaluable.

The 1% Difference is not a book about accounting or finance. It's about how companies make money and generate profit. If you are in business and want to create financial value, this book is for you!

Murray Lyons
Kelly Lyons

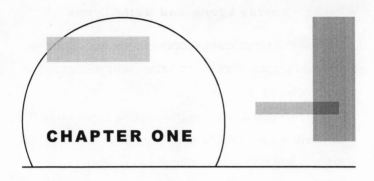

CHAPTER ONE

As it did every month, the 9x12 envelope arrived on Dave Kirkpatrick's desk a few days after month-end. No doubt, Cole Stevenson from Accounting had dropped it off before leaving for the day. The label on the front read *December Results*. A look of discouragement crept over his face. His stomach started to knot.

The damp winter cold and grey Seattle rain heightened his gloom. Outside, the rain was falling, as it often did in the middle of winter in Seattle. It was seldom cold enough to snow, but you couldn't escape the dampness. Visitors from colder climates often felt chilled, even though the air temperature was warmer than most northern states.

"Kirk," as most people called him, peered at the envelope as it lay on some papers in the middle of his desk. After years of selling, he had mastered the skill of outwardly putting a positive spin on everything. It didn't matter how good or bad the results were; whenever an outsider asked how business was, his answer was always the same—"Great!" Privately, though, worry and anxiety were the order of the day. Business was anything but great and he had lost confidence in how to initiate a turnaround for the business. He was scrambling for solutions, but nothing seemed to be working.

Piles of paper were scattered throughout Kirk's large, well-lit corner office. The computer hadn't stemmed the flow of paper one bit. On the contrary—there seemed to be more reports than ever. He leaned back in his chair, wondering how much longer this could continue. As the Branch Manager, he was ultimately responsible for branch results. Certain the report in the envelope contained little good news, his stress level soared.

Despite his best efforts, results were trending lower. Long gone were the days of high margins, growing sales, profitability and year-end bonuses. Over the past ten or fifteen years, business had changed significantly and would never be the same. While some companies prospered in this new environment, Kirk's employer, Belton's Distribution (BD), had faltered to the point where Kirk now felt that his most important career goal was simply keeping his job. The beginning of a new year was a time for change and the probability that he would be let go had just increased with the latest results. Even in a booming economy, his employment opportunities would be limited. At fifty-five, with a track record that had deteriorated for three consecutive years, Kirk knew time was running out. How times had changed since the days when he could effortlessly land a job at almost any distribution company!

BD was a family-run business with offices in six Pacific Northwest locations. The company had three main product lines—cleaning supplies, paper products and packaging materials—and distributed thousands of products. Some of their customers were retailers who resold the products to end consumers while others such as building service contractors, printers and offices used the products in their day-to-day operations.

After starting the company forty years ago, Old Man Belton had gradually expanded the business—although in the last five years he had become much less active in the day-to-day operation. Initially, he had handed his responsibilities over to his only son Doug, who he named President. Doug, however, did not have his father's business skills. After disrupting relationships with customers, suppliers and employees, it became apparent that he also didn't have the "people skills" to run the business. Eventually, Caroline Edwards, an outsider, was named President and Doug was demoted to Vice President, Operations. Doug still had an important job, but the President and Vice President of Sales were the positions with the most influence. Despite his son's lack of people skills, Old Man Belton was good to him. In any other organization, Doug would have been given a package and shown the door.

Kirk ran the Seattle branch which was situated ten minutes from the airport. Like most industrial distribution businesses, BD's offices were located in light industrial business parks where wide roads accommodated all the big rigs delivering and picking up product at the warehouses lining every street. Kirk often wondered what was inside those warehouses. He assumed there must be a market for whatever it was; otherwise, they wouldn't be there. Except for the odd café that served sandwiches, he usually had to get in his car and drive to find a decent restaurant. Nobody was out walking at lunch, and the place was deserted at night.

Kirk had been with BD for almost twenty years and had run the Seattle branch for the past ten. Just like his career as a sales rep with BD, his first six years as branch manager had been fabulous. Then the economy cratered. The first few years were hard on everyone, but Kirk managed to keep his job, despite flat sales and declining profits. While most businesses had staged a strong comeback in the last few years, BD had not recovered—a fact that Old Man Belton never let Kirk forget.

Attached to the Seattle office was the distribution centre, a big warehouse full of inventory the sales reps had to sell. Down the hall from Kirk's office were the Credit and Collections, Purchasing and Customer Service offices. At the back of the building was the warehouse manager and his staff. A constant stream of supplier trucks would unload inventory into the warehouse, where it sat until the reps sold it. Then a fleet of delivery trucks delivered the product to customers. It fell to the Purchasing department to order the right quantities of the right product and get it into the warehouse at the right time. Hopefully, the products wouldn't sit too long before they were shipped, as keeping inventory was costly. Because they often paid suppliers before their habitually slow-paying customers paid them, BD had to borrow money to finance their inventory.

Backorders complicated everything. If BD ran out of inventory or the supplier short- shipped, they were forced to backorder the customer which created extra administrative work and unrecoverable costs. With thousands of products, customers and suppliers, you can imagine how much negotiating between parties and extra work this involved. Every business has its challenges, and this was a huge challenge for BD.

Finally, after much hesitation, Kirk leaned forward, picked up the envelope and slowly pulled out the report. The first page was an income statement showing last month's results. The sales line was flat, expenses were up and profitability was down. He wasn't surprised. Despite his stoic expression, Kirk's emotions spiraled downward as he flipped to the next page to compare last year's preliminary year-end figures to those of the previous year. The trend was clear—another year of disappointing results. He had missed his most important objectives by a wide margin. His upcoming performance review would be difficult. He had a lot of explaining to do.

Looking through the large window separating his office from the open office area, Kirk could see the cubicles where the sales reps worked when they weren't on the road. The office appeared empty. It was 5:36 PM and most people had gone home for the day.

After a long period of poor performance perhaps it was time to initiate some changes with the reps. Although he had done his best to foster team spirit, Kirk was swimming against the current. It had been so long since the Seattle branch had met or exceeded goals that employees had forgotten what success felt like. The physical environment was depressing and employee turnover had increased. To add to Kirk's problems, several top sales performers had left in search of greener pastures. The employees he wanted to leave had stayed, while those he wanted to keep seemed to be leaving. No matter how bad the economy appeared to be, the best performers knew there would always be opportunities for people who were good at what they did. Consequently, the Seattle branch had only a handful of employees who exceeded expectations.

Kirk had ten outside sales reps whose responsibility was to generate results. Because they affected the biggest line on the income statement—the sales line—the reps influenced the company's results more than any other group. Sales were what BD was missing.

Despite increased competition, a few reps had still managed to grow their business. Jake Olson was one of those reps. As Jake's cubicle was one row over, Kirk couldn't see him from his office but knew he was there. Jake's black coat hung on the coat rack that stood slightly higher than his cubicle. Jake was a true professional, a people-person with an engaging smile and contagious enthusiasm. He was a team player who consistently met his targets—the type of sales rep Kirk would clone if he could. Jake seemed to have it all: a successful career, a beautiful wife named Jess, a cute little four-year-old named Michelle and a lovely home in the suburbs.

Kirk gently slid the income statement back into the envelope and filed it away. No matter how long and hard he thought about the results, he couldn't change the past. He could only change the future—and that was his plan. The branch had under performed too long! It was time to make some changes, but time was not on his side. In the coming weeks, he planned to initiate changes that would turn things around. He needed to pull BD out of mediocrity by getting more employees generating better results. After shuffling a few papers, he stood up, slipped into his raincoat and headed home.

Tomorrow was a new day.

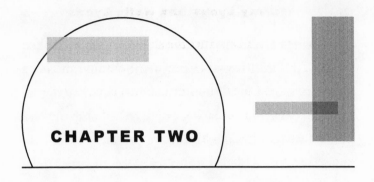

CHAPTER TWO

Steve Butler—a big man with a six-foot-four frame, two-hundred fifty pounds of muscle and a powerful voice that exuded confidence—could intimidate with little effort. While that was a huge advantage in sports, in business he had to be careful. Fortunately, he was a master at building rapport, a skill critical in sales.

Draping his long muscular arms over the top of Jake's cubicle, Steve bellowed, "How're ya doing, Jake?"

"Fantastic!" Jake replied, leaning back in his chair.

"Did you and Jess go out last night?"

"No, we decided to stay home. We ordered some pizza and after we put Michelle to bed, we watched a bit of TV."

"Great! I guess that means we can go out for a beer tonight after work. How about five o'clock at Hamptons?"

"Sounds good," Jake said.

After Steve returned to his own cubicle, Jake reached for his "To Do" list and began going through it, as he did every morning. Although he had a personal digital assistant (PDA) in his jacket pocket (the company had insisted it would make him more productive), he still preferred to scribble his notes on pieces of paper. Jake found paperwork and electronic reporting tedious and time-consuming. He estimated that 25 percent of his time went to administrative work of one form or another—time that added no apparent value to the customer. In many ways, administrative work was a competitor as it competed for time that could be better spent meeting with customers.

For every item he checked off his "To Do" list, he seemed to add three new ones. This included an e-mail from the warehouse stating they no longer stocked an item he just took an order for yesterday, a notice from Accounting that a customer was sixty days past due and one reminding him to update his Customer Relationship Management (CRM) records, etc. *Admin paperwork could eat up my whole day if I let it,* Jake thought. *We're experts in creating work that doesn't pay or create value. No wonder this company isn't growing!*

Over the last several years, BD had spent large sums of money—funds the company didn't have—supplying reps with the latest laptops, PDAs and cell phones.

Convinced that it would make the reps and the business more efficient, the company had purchased new inventory and accounting software, as well as CRM software. Trying to make his mark and take the company to the next level, Doug Belton had spent without restraint. The result was an implementation nightmare that affected every branch. After one year as President, Doug was demoted to VP, Operations and given the mandate to get the inventory system fully operational. Over the past year, the company had invested a significant amount of time and money in making all the new systems work. Snags in implementing the new inventory system had resulted in stock shortages, which in turn had led to a loss of sales and customers. The reps were frustrated, but with many of the implementation problems now behind them, they looked forward to making some headway. However, the promise of a competitive advantage had long since evaporated, as most of their competitors had adopted similar technologies.

A picture of Jess and Michelle stood beside Jake's computer monitor. Their cheerful expressions brought a moment of joy to his heart. He smiled, as thoughts of his wife and daughter brought welcome relief from the boredom of paperwork. Pinned on the wall behind the picture of his family was a large, glossy photo of the late-model BMW he had cut out of a brochure. The dream car motivated him to get out of the office and sell.

Jake loved certain aspects of selling and was good at it, but it wasn't easy. Aware that rejection was part of a sales rep's life, the company provided various incentives—trips, bonuses and commission—to create motivation and drive sales. Unfortunately, one of the downsides of the Sales Department's incentives was that employees in other parts of the organization often felt neglected.

Ten outside sales reps worked in the large open office area where Jake worked. Karen Briere, "the chatterbox," occupied the cubicle directly behind him. Her constant chatter disrupted Jake to the point where he was sometimes forced to do office work in the solitude of his home. Karen was young, attractive and single. Her long blonde hair and blue eyes captivated almost all the guys in the office—even those who weren't single. Jake wisely kept his distance, maintaining a friendly professional relationship with the attractive young woman, despite her annoying chatter. Always appearing busy, Karen used administration work as her excuse for not being able to sell more.

Shortly after lunch, Jim Hayward from Purchasing stopped by Jake's desk to discuss a special product Jake wanted him to bring in for a new customer. Jim had started in the warehouse right after college and had gradually worked his way into Purchasing. Jim, Jake and Steve had become good friends while playing on the same ball team.

"The customer's currently small, but they've got good future potential," explained Jake.

"I'll bring the product in," Jim said, "if you can get approval from Kirk."

"Okay, thanks. By the way, Steve and I are going for a beer after work. Care to join us?"

Jim readily accepted the invitation.

Later that day, Jake left the office and stepped out into the damp West Coast air. It was chilly and raining slightly, but the air was refreshing. After drowning in paperwork all day, Jake felt the need to get out of the office and have a beer. He felt his energy returning as he walked across the dimly lit parking lot to his domestic four-door sedan. "This car's certainly no BMW! It's got "traveling salesman" written all over it," Jake mumbled to himself as he slid into the driver's seat. His car allowance would never cover the cost of his dream car.

After a few minutes of driving down several warehouse-lined streets, Jake exited the light industrial area and entered the shopping district beside a residential area on the other side of the freeway. Just ahead of him was the Hamptons Pub sign. It was 5:00 PM when Jake squeezed the big sedan into a tight parking spot, carefully opened his door and stepped out, mindful of the car beside him.

Hamptons sports bar was crowded by the time Jake arrived. It was always busy whenever happy hour coincided with a big game and a two-for-one wings special, and tonight was no exception. Some patrons stood around small, round, chest-high tables, while others sat on chairs around rectangular oak tables. Multiple, strategically-placed, large-screen TVs hung from the ceiling, allowing patrons to watch several sporting events at a time. Sports paraphernalia adorned the walls. Behind the bartenders were shelves stocked with every type of liquor imaginable. Above the shelves, a large chalkboard advertised the food and drink specials.

As Jake weaved through the crowd, he spotted Jim and Steve, who had somehow managed to get a window table. They were both seated with pints of beer in front of them. An extra pint sat in front of the empty seat they had saved for him.

"Hey guys, how're you doing?" Jake said, sitting down.

Steve grinned. "What could be better than cheap wings and a couple beers with my buddies? What a great way to start the New Year!"

The three friends raised their glasses and said in unison, "Cheers!"

After some small talk, the three colleagues discussed business. "What kind of a year do you think we'll have, Steve?" Jim asked.

"It should be great. It's a new year," Steve replied.

Jim was not convinced. "We've had several years of flat sales and declining profits. I'm not so sure we'll be able to pull out of it this time."

"Well, I'd like to be optimistic, but I guess the odds aren't in our favor," Steve confessed. "It seems we're working harder and harder to generate the same sales, less profit and, worst of all, less commission. Something has to change, but I'm not sure what it is."

"I think BD needs to make some management changes," Jim said. "You guys know what it's like in sports. If the team doesn't perform well, the coach is fired first. Kirk is a great guy, but the world is changing and he keeps trying to make it work the old way. He was effective in the past, but business is different today. Offshore products are making it tough for us to compete, on-line auctions are driving prices down and our competitors' service is better than ever. Look at that new online distribution company with the warehouse in Portland—it has a huge inside sales force and a great website that customers can use to place their orders anytime, day or night. They don't even have an outside sales force. They just keep working the phones, promoting the website and offering everyday low prices. Their cost structure is a lot lower than ours. We're having a tough time beating them in our own market! How can we possibly compete with them?"

Jake agreed and hoped he wouldn't be affected by any changes Kirk might make. With his wife expecting in a few months, he needed to find a way to grow sales and make more money. Jess was planning to give up her job and stay at home with the children.

As if reading Jake's thoughts, Steve said, "We could never survive on just one income. How will you and Jess be able to swing it?"

"I don't know, Steve," Anxious to change the subject, Jake directed the conversation back to work. "Do you think BD should lower prices, expand product selection and play the volume game?"

"Do you think that would work for us?" Steve queried.

"Why not?" Jake replied. "It works for the big box retailers. Imagine how much more we could sell if we lowered our prices by 10%-15%. We'd kill the competition, including that new distributor with the inside sales force and fancy website."

"All the extra suppliers and volume would certainly add new challenges to my job," Jim commented.

All three colleagues agreed that cutting price was the best way to grow the business.

"Guys, let's wait until tomorrow to change the world," Steve piped up. "The game's starting. Let's order some more wings and another round!"

Despite the cold beer, the company of good friends and sports on TV, Jake couldn't shake the unease of not knowing how the year would proceed. He was already feeling the pressure of rising expenses and the imminent loss of Jess's income.

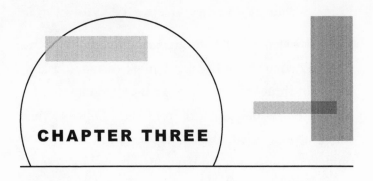

CHAPTER THREE

The next morning, as usual, Jake began his day at the office by checking his email. His heart skipped a beat, as he read an e-mail from Kirk marked "Urgent." Headed by a short subject line—Sales Results—and addressed to all sales reps, the message read, "You are required to attend a meeting this Friday at 8:00 AM in the conference room to review last year's results and your sales forecast for the coming year. Attendance is mandatory!"

Jake knew the meeting would not be pleasant. Kirk obviously wasn't happy. The entire sales team immediately began to speculate about what would happen. Everyone knew the previous year had been another soft one with flat sales and declining profits. The e-mail created a new level of seriousness and urgency. The reps knew it was their responsibility as the company's front line to grow the business, but for a variety of reasons that hadn't happened.

Kirk's demeanor had changed over the past two years. Previously, he had been more casual and laid-back, but things were different now. No doubt, he was under tremendous pressure from Head Office to turn things around. He had tried new sales initiatives, new products, new markets and training, but nothing seemed to work. Employee turnover had increased and morale was low. Was the writing on the wall? Was BD destined to sink slowly into the ground, to be remembered only as a once thriving business that had lost its edge to more innovative and aggressive competitors? Jake wondered where everyone would end up and, more importantly, what his fate would be. He knew that unprofitable businesses usually didn't survive.

Jake had barely finished reading the e-mail when his phone rang. Although Steve was on the road, he already knew about Kirk's e-mail.

"Did you read the message from Kirk?" Steve inquired.

"Yes, it didn't take long to read."

"What do you make of it? Steve asked."

"I think we're going to get the 'lousy results' speech again," Jake said.

"How long is this going to go on?" lamented Steve. "Doesn't Kirk realize that coming down hard on us isn't working?"

In a comforting voice Jake responded. "Senior management is probably coming down even harder on him and he's cracking."

"You and I grew sales last year by 5%-10%. Do you think we'll be okay?" Steve asked worriedly.

"If Kirk focuses on sales growth, we should be okay, but if he focuses on profitability, we'll probably get targeted like everyone else."

"I've got to go," Steve said. "My call starts in a few minutes. Talk to you later."

Because he had gone for a beer with the boys the previous night, Jake made a point of arriving home on time that evening. Jess was cooking dinner and Michelle was playing at the neighbor's house. Jess was a fantastic mother and a great wife. Like every couple, they had problems, but always seemed to resolve them. Jess came from a good family, which, from Jake's perspective, was one of the reasons she was so well grounded. She had grown up in a middle-class family with a stay-at-home mom and a dad who worked very hard as a manager in an insurance office.

Both Jake and Jess felt it would be preferable for her to stay home with Michelle and their second child, who was due soon. But the loss of Jess's income would create more financial pressures. They faced a difficult decision.

"Hi Jake! How was your day?" Jess asked cheerfully as he walked in the door.

"It was okay. Kirk called a meeting for this Friday to review last year's results, which were below target. No one wants to go, but he made it quite clear attendance was mandatory."

Jess already had a worried look on her face. "Should we be concerned about your future with BD?"

"No, I'm sure I'll be fine," he said reassuringly. "It's just a difficult period for the company. Don't worry, everything will be alright."

Jess looked relieved, but deep down Jake was not. Jess had a tendency to worry too much, so Jake often painted a more optimistic picture for his wife and kept the worrisome details to himself. As a result, he often felt alone.

Jake had trouble sleeping the Thursday night before the meeting. He tossed and turned, unable to get his mind off the meeting Kirk had scheduled for the next morning. His mind skipped from one thought to another. Every half hour or so, he looked at the large digital display on the alarm clock and thought about how tired he'd be in the morning if he didn't get to sleep immediately. Finally, at about 3:00 A.M., he slipped into a light sleep. A few hours later, he dragged himself out of bed and got ready for work. After picking up a very large cup of coffee on the way, he was in the office by 7:00 AM.

Before the meeting began, Jake reviewed his forecast several times. Although he couldn't change last year's results, he could change his forecast. Working carefully through his customer list, he thought about every option for increasing sales. Last year he had grown sales by 7 percent, and this year he was forecasting another 3 percent growth. Sensing this was not enough to please Kirk, he felt compelled to bump up the numbers to show a 10 percent increase. BD always welcomed forecasts of double-digit increases that were justified with a plan of action. In the end, he concluded it would be better to raise his forecast now and worry about selling later. After all, he had one year to achieve the target, which he concluded could be reached by working harder. He realized this tactic had the potential to backfire if he couldn't deliver. In fact, Kirk and Purchasing would also look bad if they ordered product based on a faulty forecast and ended up with excess inventory. Jake new the plan was risky, but it would alleviate some of his immediate stress.

A few minutes before 8:00 AM, all the reps filed down the long, dingy hallway to the boardroom. The motivational and product posters pinned on the wall only served as painful reminders that no one was motivated and that many of the products they promoted rarely sold. It was a sore reminder of the state of their business. Employees in Customer Service, Purchasing and other areas all waited eagerly on the outside for the inside scoop. They knew what was happening, but luckily for them, they weren't the ones on trial.

None of the sales reps ever met with customers in the dilapidated boardroom. Like the rest of the office, the room was dated and in desperate need of renovation. The vintage '80s chairs were shabby and the large solid-wood conference table, which stretched from one end of the room to the other, was in dire need of refinishing. On a table in the back corner sat a relic from the past—an overhead projector. With the advent of laptops and computer projectors, such old technology was redundant, but for some reason BD had insisted on keeping it. The same paintings had graced the walls for twenty years. On more than one occasion, employees had asked for renovations, but the response from management was always the same: "We don't have the money in this year's budget." Several years ago, Kirk had allocated funds for renovations, but when it became apparent that sales had plummeted, management quickly slashed the renovation budget to zero. *Everything* hinged on sales.

Everyone, including Jake, took their usual seats in the boardroom. Several reps nervously joked about the fact that no one ever changed their seats. Jake laughed, but couldn't help thinking to himself, *They're right. Why don't we even want to change where we sit?* Soon the joking subsided and an uneasy silence, broken periodically by the odd comment, swept through the room. There was tension in the air; everyone knew this would be an uncomfortable meeting. Although Kirk hadn't yet arrived, it was obvious he had been in the room earlier, since his laptop was already connected to the projector. The opening slide was entitled "Last Year's Results."

A hush descended upon the room again at precisely 8:00 AM when Kirk entered. Without saying a word, he slowly shut the door and locked it—even though one of the reps, Pam Christopherson, was absent. Her constant tardiness bothered Kirk, but he had never locked her out before. Kirk didn't have to ask the sales reps for their attention—he already had it. Jake glanced across the table at Steve, noticing that he was nervously playing with his pen. Even Karen the chatterbox was quiet. The locked door accentuated the seriousness of the meeting.

Kirk opened the meeting with his usual complimentary remark, which this morning seemed forced. "Thanks for coming today. We have two items on the agenda this morning—the review of last year's results and this year's forecast. Let's begin with last year's results."

He pressed the forward button on his remote and brought up a simplified income statement. It was just a few weeks after year-end, so the reps knew the statement wasn't the final version. Kirk remained silent as he looked at the slide, which read:

Year End Comparative Income Statement

	Previous Year	% to Sales	Last Year	% to Sales
Sales	$29,638,000		$29,700,000	
Cost of Goods Sold	21,467,000	72.4%	21,600,000	72.7%
Gross Profit	8,171,000	27.6%	8,100,000	27.3%
Expenses	7,598,000	25.6%	7,722,000	26.0%
Pre Tax Income	$ 573,000	1.9%	$ 378,000	1.3%

Turning to the group, Kirk asked, "What do these numbers tell you?"

No one wanted to say anything; they were too embarrassed. A knock on the door broke the silence. Jake instantly felt rescued by the interruption, but Kirk didn't move. The knocking continued but Kirk stood motionless, peering into the eyes of the reps. *What's going on?* Jake wondered. What kind of message was Kirk trying to send?

Jake's eyes darted between Kirk and the door. He wondered what would happen next. No one knew what to do. Everybody assumed it was Pam trying unsuccessfully to open the door. Finally, Karen asked Kirk if he wanted her to answer the door. Kirk replied, "I'm not expecting anyone else."

"What about Pam?" Karen asked.

"Yesterday was Pam's last day with us," Kirk said. "She didn't want me to announce it until today. I was going to tell you this morning. Whoever is at the door most likely wants to deliver a message, but it can wait. We're in the middle of a meeting. These interruptions have been happening too often and I want to put an end to them. From now on, we will run our meetings differently. We will start on time and finish on time with no interruptions and no phone calls. So if your cell is on right now, I suggest you turn it off. " In the past, the reps would often take calls during team meetings, but now a melody of tones sounded as everyone quickly reached for their cell phones to turn them off.

The news of Pam's departure stunned everyone in the room. In the eighteen months she had been with BD she had not produced great results, but she had been new to the industry. Some had questioned her attitude—instead of focusing on what initiatives she could take to make BD a better company, she had presented reasons why she couldn't produce, often pointing a finger at other people and telling them what they were doing wrong. She had been the only person opposed to the new CRM system and had refused to try to make it work.

Jake had not realized Pam's job security had been threatened. It appeared Kirk was trying to make a fresh start. He had to admit that getting rid of an underperformer like Pam and setting new ground rules for meetings was long overdue.

"Can you buy into the new meeting format?" Kirk asked the group. Everyone quickly nodded. No one was about to oppose Kirk today.

"Good! Then let's get back to my question. What do these numbers tell you?"

Jake felt compelled to speak. "Overall, the numbers don't paint a good picture. Sales are flat while cost of goods sold and expenses both increased by roughly $100,000 each. The net result is that pre-tax income was almost cut in half."

"That's a good summary, Jake," Kirk said. "What do you think will happen this year if the trend continues?"

"We'll have no profit and our third or fourth year of zero growth," Jake replied.

"Exactly. The last few years have been rough, but this year will be..." Kirk paused to stare intently at the group.

"Much better!" Jake responded.

"I sure hope so," Kirk said, "because with results like these, this branch is not viable. Given the millions BD has invested in us, we are not providing much of a return. Quite frankly, they'd be better off selling the business or shutting us down and investing the money in the bond market where they can earn a risk-free return that's higher than what we give them today. No one wants to see that happen."

He clicked onto his next slide. "Nonetheless, we had a few bright spots last year. Jane Winston, Steve Butler and Jake Olson and all grew sales by more than 5 percent, with Jane increasing sales by 14 percent. Congratulations, Jane! In addition, all of you played a part in the successful introduction of our new XL line in Q4. Finally, we introduced a new inventory management system, which should help reduce costs this coming year. It created a lot of headaches last year, but you all supported the change and tried to make it work."

There wasn't much positive news from last year, but Kirk mentioned all of it. The tone of the meeting started to improve. With the press of a button, up came the final slide, which read, "Thanks for your participation. The next sales meeting is scheduled for Jan 27 at 8:00 AM."

Assuming Kirk had forgotten about the final item on the agenda, Steve asked, "What about our sales forecasts you asked for?"

"For us to survive in the long run, we need a major change and a breakout year," Kirk explained. "We need to set and achieve *stretch* goals, not your typical realistic goals. I'm guessing the forecasts you have sitting in front of you right now are solid, well-thought-out, realistic goals, forecasting increases in the 3%-5% range. That's not enough, so rather than put any one person on the spot, I want to give everyone a chance to adjust their numbers before going public with them. It's going to be tough on you and everyone else in the office, but it's what we need to do. We're running out of time and options. Bring your numbers to the next meeting, along with your rationale on how you plan to achieve your stretch goal. Are there any other questions?" As there was none, Kirk thanked the reps for their time and left the boardroom.

Silence prevailed in the room again, but for different reasons. The meeting had lasted only fifteen minutes, but more had happened in that meeting than in any other Jake could remember. Kirk had communicated volumes, even though only two slides contained information and only four people had spoken. News of Pam's departure had floored them; they had received a tough message; and Kirk had challenged them—yet, hardly a word was spoken! The reps sat stunned like deer in headlights on a dark night.

Although only the sales reps had attended the meeting, within minutes everyone in the office knew what had transpired during the meeting. Employees from other departments were desperate for information. The usual office buzz was replaced with quiet side conversations and speculation about what would happen next and who else might be fired. Nobody knew what to think or do. Some employees left the office. Clearly, things had changed. Within fifteen short minutes, the winds of change had unexpectedly blown in, leaving everyone feeling as though they were walking on thin ice, praying they wouldn't fall through as Pam had. Turning BD around just became a lot more important.

Jake tried to work, but he couldn't take his mind off the morning's events. Not wanting to talk to customers, he forwarded his calls to voicemail. At lunchtime, he received an e-mail from Steve, which read, "Let's get out of here and go to Hamptons." Jake immediately hit the reply button and said he would be there in ten minutes.

The office was almost empty when Jake left. Obviously, others were also looking to escape the tense atmosphere to help them deal with whatever changes they thought might happen. At times like these, everyone speculates, and most of the time that's all it is—speculation about events that never occur. Anxiety replaces complacency and a feeling of insecurity takes hold, like a sickness with no cure. Jake tried to convince himself that it wasn't as bad as it felt.

Hamptons was always busy at lunchtime on Fridays. Jake saw Steve sitting in a poorly lit corner near the pool table. They weren't the only BD employees there; across the room was a table of four or five office staff. Preferring to keep to themselves, Steve and Jake pretended not to notice them. The lunch hour extended into the early afternoon, as Steve and Jake discussed everything from morale and inventory problems to increased competition. They concluded that the grass looked a lot greener pretty much everywhere else—BD was no longer a fun place to work.

After a few beers, Steve picked up his cell phone as if making a call and spoke dramatically into the phone,

"Kirk, I just wanted to let you know that this afternoon I'm not available for you, for your stinking company or customers. Have a nice day!" With that, he dropped the phone on the table, and he and Jake had a good laugh.

Not to be outdone, Jake picked up his phone and in a loud, booming voice began singing, "Take this job and shove it. I ain't working here no more . . ." In one fluid motion, Jake folded the flip-phone shut and threw it on the table, as both he and Steve leaned back in their chairs, howling with laughter. Humor is a great healer and their mood greatly improved as the afternoon progressed—perhaps a little *too* much. By the time they realized they had spent the entire afternoon sitting in the pub blowing off steam and telling stories, it was already four o'clock. The last time Jake had spent an entire afternoon in a pub had been back in college.

Both Jake and Steve were in no shape to go back to work. In sales, it was easy to go missing for a few hours—co-workers assumed they were out making calls. Jake and Steve at least had the common sense to call a cab to take them home.

When Jake's cab pulled up in front of his house, Jess was walking Michelle home from the neighbor's house. His timing couldn't have been worse. As he paid the cabbie, Jake desperately searched for a way to explain why he had taken a cab home. It was time to go into selling mode.

Unaware of what was going on, Michelle asked innocently, "Daddy, where's your car?"

"Well, I decided not to bring it home tonight."

"Why?"

"Because I wasn't feeling good," Jake said, "and I thought it would be safer not to drive in case I got sick."

"Does your tummy hurt?"

"Yes, and my head, too."

"I'll take care of you, Daddy," Michelle said helpfully. "I'll be the doctor and you can be my patient."

"Okay, that sounds good to me."

As he stumbled up the walkway, Jess leaned over and whispered angrily, "You smell like a brewery! What's going on, and where's the car?"

"The car's fine . . . and more than you can imagine happened today. Let me play with Michelle for twenty minutes and then we can talk."

As soon as they entered the house, Jess said to Michelle, "I have to talk to Daddy while you set up your doctor's office. I'll send him into your room in a few minutes so you can play doctor."

Jess pulled Jake into the kitchen as the eager little doctor skipped down the hallway. "What happened?" she demanded to know.

It didn't take long for Jake to recount the events of the morning's sales meeting with Kirk. As he left for his appointment with Michelle, Jess asked in a concerned voice, "What does this mean to us?"

"I wish I knew," Jake replied. Without thinking, he had broken his habit of shielding Jess from his worries.

That night, Jake nervously paced around the house. He couldn't relax and watch TV or keep himself occupied with a hobby or a book. Tormented by his worries about the future, he felt sick. Reminding himself that change was seldom as bad as it seemed provided little relief. Jake was proud of the fact that he could keep negative emotions in check, but it wasn't working tonight. Whenever a creative idea popped into his head, two or three negative thoughts quickly replaced it. He couldn't get off his emotional rollercoaster.

As Jake walked aimlessly around the house searching for something to calm his nerves, he recalled a conversation he'd had two months earlier with his friend Tom Sinclair. When Tom's company had downsized, his manager had arranged a ten-minute meeting with everyone in the office one Friday afternoon. During those ten minutes, employees were advised if they had a job in the new restructured organization. If they didn't, he went over their severance package and then asked them to leave. They had to hand over their access key, employee ID, cell phone, laptop and PDA. Their personal belongings would be couriered to them the following day. Finally, they were escorted out of the building to a cab that was waiting out front. Tom said employees knew the procedure because another office had done the same thing a week earlier. Anxious about how many people would be fired that day, employees counted the cabs waiting on the main street below. Before the Friday morning meeting, Jake couldn't imagine this happening at BD, but now anything seemed possible.

Saturday morning arrived soon enough. Feeling guilty about his lack of productivity the previous day, Jake forced himself to do a little work. When he opened his emails, one from Kirk immediately caught his attention. Dated 4:00 PM on Friday, it read, "I wanted to meet briefly with you this afternoon. Please stop by my office for ten minutes at 8:30 AM on Monday morning."

What's wrong now? Jake wondered. *Why didn't Kirk give me more information about this meeting?*

Weekends usually passed quickly for Jake, but this one seemed never-ending. Saturday afternoon dragged into a sleepless Saturday night. Drained and exhausted, he finally fell asleep Sunday afternoon watching the game. For two hours he slept in the comfort of his big leather chair beside the dimmed lamp with the TV on in the background. Sleep and a fresh perspective were just what he needed.

On the drive to work Monday morning, Jake wondered what was in store for him. Over the weekend, he had imagined every possibility, both good and bad, but hadn't arrived at any logical conclusion. He had worked hard to convince himself that his sales results for the past year made him safe, but his emotions were trying to convince him otherwise.

As Jake approached Kirk's corner office, he saw that his boss's door was ajar. Out of respect, Jake knocked.

"Come in, Jake," Kirk said cordially. "Have a seat." Kirk was working on his computer. With the exception of a plain white #10 envelope directly in front of him, his desk was unusually clean. Jack's name was printed in bold capital letters on the envelope's label. Off to the side were several similar envelopes sitting face down on top of a small stack of papers.

Leaning forward, Kirk pushed the envelope toward Jake. "This is what I wanted to talk to you about on Friday afternoon," he said. Hesitantly, Jake reached for the unsealed envelope, which Kirk urged him to open.

Jake reached in and pulled out two letter-sized sheets of paper folded in three. He nervously unfolded the paper. He couldn't believe his eyes—inside were five crisp, one-hundred dollar bills! The first piece of paper was an airline e-ticket for two to Las Vegas; the second was a confirmation for three nights' accommodation at Caesar's Palace.

Stunned, Jake asked, "What's this for?"

Rising, Kirk extended his hand. "It's for your contribution last year. You were one of the top three reps in sales dollar growth. We don't do a very good job at recognizing people around here, so on Friday at lunch I went out and bought three trips—one for you, Steve and Jane. I know Friday morning was tough. I felt like I needed to send a message, but I wanted to balance it with recognition where recognition is due. Please don't mention anything about the trip to anyone until I've met with the others. Congratulations again, and thanks for your contribution."

As Jake walked out of the office with his envelope in hand, he saw Steve waiting to enter Kirk's office for his meeting. He was unusually quiet and looked very nervous.

"Don't worry, it's good!" Jake said softly.

Within ten minutes, Steve was at Jake's cubicle, envelope in hand. "Do you believe it? I can't believe old

Kirk did that for us. Here we were sitting in the pub on Friday afternoon bashing the boss, while he was out buying us trips to Vegas!"

"I know. I'm feeling pretty foolish right now," Jake said. "A ruined weekend, no sleep and all those thoughts racing through my head about what I might have to do in the future . . . and all that time I had nothing to worry about. I still can't believe it."

"Well, believe it, Jake. We're going to Vegas. It's party time!"

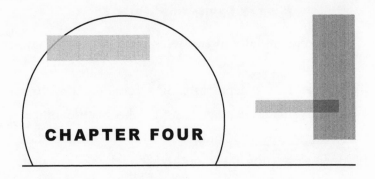

CHAPTER FOUR

Kirk didn't make it to the next sales meeting. BD let him go just days before the meeting. The official reason for his departure was "early retirement," but given the poor performance of the past several years, everyone knew that "early retirement" was code for "fired." Jake hoped Kirk had received a decent severance package, since he was near retirement and had given many good years to BD. Kirk was like a professional athlete who had struggled to keep playing years after he should have retired. *Too bad he had to go out on such a low note*, Jake mused.

Ironically, Kirk had regained some respect—he had dealt with a performance problem, was intent on making the meetings more productive and had provided increased recognition and rewards with the Vegas trips. In the end, though, it was "too little too late" In the last few years, Kirk hadn't created any financial value for the company. The game was over for Kirk. He became the second casualty in two weeks and Jake never saw him again.

After Kirk's departure, BD's president Caroline Edwards made regular trips to the Seattle office, meeting with reps and office staff to ensure that things were running smoothly. She emphasized that growing sales and profits were essential—an old story with which Jake and the others were all too familiar. Fortunately, knowing that a new manager would soon be in place, Caroline had the wisdom not to initiate too many changes. Although Head Office did not make an announcement, people speculated that Jane, the top rep, was in line for the job. Jake and others were convinced they could do the job, but senior management didn't open the position up to internal employees, and no employee was given an opportunity to discuss his or her desire to fill the position. BD was obviously looking for an outsider—someone who could make things happen.

Then in mid-February, an e-mail from Caroline Edwards announced that Scott Johnson would assume the role of branch manager, effective March 1 and that he and his family would be relocating from Dallas. Scott had extensive distribution experience, having held positions in sales, operations and finance. Caroline was excited about having Scott join the team and looked forward to his arrival. Given Kirk's replacement was found so soon suggested that the search for a new branch manager may have begun before Kirk was fired, but that was of little concern now.

In the ensuing weeks, anticipation grew as to what Scott would be like, the changes he would make and if he were a "people person" or a "numbers guy." Head Office provided sparse details, so the employees in the Seattle branch waited in suspense. Kirk had not been the best of managers in recent years, but at least they had known what to expect from him. Although they knew very little about their new leader, everyone was aware that Scott Johnson's arrival on March 1 would herald changes.

At 8:00 AM on March 1, Scott arrived with Caroline Edwards. After escorting him through the office, casually introducing him to those who were there, she spent most of the day with him in Kirk's old office going over past results, systems and processes. She called a formal meeting at 5:00 PM to introduce Scott to everyone who was available.

At 5:00 PM, everyone crowded into the conference room for the formal introduction. There was seating for twenty people but twenty-eight attended, so some had to stand at the back. Jake found the meeting very predictable—a thank-you for attending; nice welcoming remarks from the president, along with a few words to say how excited she was to have Scott join the company; and finally some kind remarks from Scott about what a great opportunity it was and how excited he was to join the company, followed by a few questions from employees.

The following morning, Scott sent an e-mail to all staff. Entitled "Update," the message read, "Please schedule a thirty-minute meeting with me over the next week to update me on your activities and projects. If you're part of the sales team, bring your forecast along as well. Finally, block off 3:00 PM to 4:00 PM on March 10 for a staff meeting in the conference room."

Jake and Steve concluded that while this seemed like a reasonable approach for Scott to update himself on what everyone was doing, the schedule seemed aggressive. Meeting with thirty employees in one week on top of all the other work was a big undertaking.

Jake scheduled his meeting with Scott for the morning of March 10. Steve wanted to get it over as soon as possible, so he booked his meeting for March 3.

Office gossip about Scott spread as people gathered details about their new manager. Although most had a good impression, a few weren't so sure. Still others thought they should have been in line for the job. Since these people felt Scott had taken their job, they would be more difficult for Scott to win over. The crazy thing was that a couple of the people who felt they were in line for a promotion were just average performers. Rather than first proving their value to the company, they thought they should have been promoted so they could show how good they were. They didn't seem to understand that you have to demonstrate your value first.

Jake's cell phone rang as he drove down the interstate the morning of March 3. It was Steve; he had just finished his meeting with Scott. After a quick hello, Jake asked him how the meeting went.

"Fantastic!" Steve exclaimed. "Scott seemed genuinely interested in what I was doing. He also asked how I felt about BD and what I thought needed to change in order for the company to succeed. He was very supportive and asked if I needed his help on any accounts. I was impressed."

"That sounds encouraging," Jake said, relieved. "I guess I don't have to be concerned about the meeting."

"Not at all, Jake. You're going to be fine."

"I'll see you later this afternoon when I return to the office."

At four o'clock, after finishing his sales calls, Jake turned into the BD parking lot, pulling up beside a late-model black BMW with Texas plates. It had to be Scott's car. *The guy's got taste*, Jake thought. It wasn't the same model as the picture hanging in his cubicle, but it was the right brand. Perhaps he had more in common with Scott than he had initially thought.

Most of Jake's colleagues had finished for the day and were heading home when he walked into the office. It didn't take long to learn that Scott had left a positive impression. Karen and Jim gave the same feedback Steve had provided—that Scott was genuinely interested in people.

As Jake was taking off his coat, Scott happened to walk by. "Did you have a good day, Jake?" he enquired.

"Yes, very good, thanks!" Jake was impressed that Scott had remembered his name.

"Excellent! I'm looking forward to meeting with you next week. I understand you were one of the top performers last year."

"Yes, I was lucky enough to increase sales last year."

"I believe selling takes more skill than luck, Jake, but however it happened, you got the job done. Nice car, by the way!" Scott added, pointing to the picture of the BMW on Jake's cubicle wall. As quickly as Scott appeared he was gone, continuing down the hallway toward Purchasing.

Jake stood motionless for a minute, thinking about his interaction with Scott. The man had obviously done his homework over the last few days and probably knew more about what was going on in the company than people gave him credit for. Jake concluded he had better be as prepared as Scott for his upcoming meeting with him. After checking messages and processing a few orders, Jake headed home less than an hour later.

Only ten days had passed since everyone had crammed into the conference room to meet Scott for the first time. Now they were meeting again for their first branch meeting with Scott. Shoulder to shoulder they sat or stood in the tight quarters. Given their positive first impression of the new branch manager, everyone had looked forward to the meeting. They wouldn't be disappointed.

"Thanks for coming," Scott said, opening the meeting. "It's been great meeting with you this past week to learn more about what you do, the challenges we face and, more importantly, what some of the solutions might be. I'd like to begin with two important announcements."

Jake's thoughts raced, as Scott paused briefly. *Here it comes,* Jake thought, *the big change!* Reaching down, Scott slowly picked up his black leather portfolio and pulled out a single white envelope. Fear in the eyes and minds of some instantly transformed to excitement. By now, the "envelope" story was famous in the office; everyone had a good idea as to what was inside, but no one knew who the recipient would be.

In a clear, confident manner, Scott continued. "At the beginning of the year, an envelope like this was given to each of the three sales reps who grew sales last year. As you know, that's a key goal, so recognition was due; however, one other person deserves equal recognition." He paused to glance around the room. The anticipation escalated.

"This envelope goes to the person who generated the most gross profit dollars last year. For those of you who don't know, gross profit is what's left over when you take the sales line and subtract the cost of goods sold (COGS) for those sales. That person is Sue Ho. Congratulations, Sue!" Everyone applauded as an astonished Sue rose and walked over to Scott to receive the envelope. Scott shook her hand warmly.

Sue was different from most BD reps. Quiet and easygoing, she rarely socialized with the other reps. Some office staff and reps had labeled her as ineffective and not a team player, but Jake saw her as an average performer who preferred to keep to herself.

Scott's second announcement was also unexpected. "I'm inviting each of you to a dinner at Vic's Steakhouse next Thursday after work. It's BD's way of saying thank you for your hard work last year in getting the new computer system up and running." The room erupted in cheers and applause. Since they seldom received recognition for their contribution to the company, the office staff was especially excited.

Although the last forty minutes of the meeting were less eventful, everyone left in good spirits. With the exception of a few people who were still skeptical about Scott's approach, the buzz was positive. Some still believed he was trying to win people over before he delivered the bad news—whatever that may be.

The following week passed quickly and before they knew it, Jake and Steve were driving to Vic's Steakhouse, a Seattle landmark known for quality food and reasonable prices. Scott had reserved the private dining room, which had seating for thirty five — just enough to seat all the employees if everyone showed up. Jake noticed all the wine bottles, beer and margaritas; some people were obviously taking advantage of the fact that drinks were on the house. At the end of the table was Karen, looking outstanding as usual, surrounded by several guys. The steak and salmon arrived steaming hot and cooked to perfection. Jake realized that events like this helped to build employee morale, which may have been Scott's intention. In the past, employees got together only once a year—for lunch at Christmas—so this was special.

After everyone had eaten, Scott stood up to say a few words. "I'd like to thank everyone for coming tonight. I hope your meal was as good as mine. The purpose of this dinner was to recognize your contribution in getting our new computer system operational. It's much more work than meets the eye—doing inventory, loading thousands of products into the system, the pricing for all those products, our customer contract pricing terms, and on and on it goes. I guess I don't have to tell you how much work it is, because you did it.

"Anytime a new manager takes over, people usually wonder what changes will be made, especially if the branch hasn't produced the results Corporate expects. Understandably, this causes stress and tension, which some of you may be feeling. There is no question we have to improve our results, but I want you to know that I won't be investing any time in planning significant changes. I think we can turn things around by year-end with the people in this room.

"All of you are important to BD," Scott continued. "Otherwise, you wouldn't have been hired. Everyday you make important decisions that are reflected on our income statement. These decisions come in many forms—from how much we pay for fuel to purchasing product to managing inventory to selling the product and, finally, collecting money. Hopefully, we *do* collect our money! You—not I—make these decisions, so in many ways it's your branch, not mine. One of my top priorities will be to spend time with you individually and as a group to help you understand the difference that small, 1 percent changes have on our business. One percent may not sound like much, but believe me, it has the power to transform this business. So, let's raise our glasses to a great year. *It's turnaround time!*"

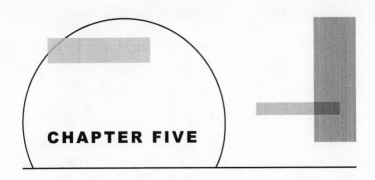

CHAPTER FIVE

The call arrived the morning of March 23. "Hi, Jake. It's Tim Saunders calling," said the voice at the other end. Tim was a purchasing agent for Sunrise Grocery, a local chain with about fifteen mid-sized stores. The big players hadn't squeezed them out of the market yet, because they had quality products and a family atmosphere. The original owner was still working in the business fifty years after opening his first location at Fifth and Main.

"Good to hear from you, Tim," Jake said. "How are you doing?"

"Excellent, thanks."

"That's great! How can I help you?"

"Well, I was hoping we could meet to discuss our business," Tim replied. "We're making some changes around here, and there's an opportunity for you to earn more of our business. Do you have some time in the next few days?"

"That's the kind of meeting I can make time for . . . how about Thursday afternoon?"

"Can we make it 3:00 PM?" Tim suggested.

"Consider it booked. I'll see you then." Jake was so excited he forgot to ask Tim how much extra business he had in mind, what products were involved, when the change would take effect and pretty much every other question he should have asked. At least he wouldn't have to wait long to learn the details.

Jake arrived on time for his meeting with Tim. The receptionist escorted him into a small office where Tim joined him five minutes later. A fancy plaque on the wall listed the Sunrise Grocery corporate values regarding quality and service. After the usual small talk, Jake and Tim got right down to business. Tim explained the pressures his company was facing. With mega stores establishing a presence in the community, it was becoming more difficult to remain competitive. At some point, customers would switch because of price. Jake couldn't argue with that—Jess did most of their shopping at the mega stores. They shopped at Sunrise only when they wanted fresh, high-quality produce or meat. Tim stated he had no choice but to follow the same cost-cutting strategy the mega stores used with their suppliers. While he liked dealing with BD, he had to find a way to lower costs. He was prepared to increase

BD's business from $100,000 to $130,000 if Jake lowered his prices by 7 percent.

Jake quickly concluded that 30 percent higher volume would more than offset the 7 percent discount; nonetheless, he would still try to negotiate a higher price. Jake began by offering a 3 percent discount, knowing it wouldn't be enough. He wanted to leave with an agreement in hand, so after fifteen minutes of negotiation, he agreed to give Sunrise 5 percent with an additional 2 percent discount if they paid within thirty days. Jake happily walked out the door with an additional $30,000 worth of business.

The next morning when Jake told Scott he had received a commitment from Sunrise for an additional $30,000 of business Scott responded.

"That's fantastic! Was it at current margins?"

"Not exactly," Jake replied. "They're experiencing intense competition from the mega stores. We'd likely lose all their business if we didn't reduce our price by 7 percent. In the end, I gave them 5 percent off the top, and to earn the final 2 percent, they have to pay within thirty days."

"That's quite a discount. How long do they take to pay their bills now?"

"Thirty-five days."

"What do you think the impact will be on our profitability?" Scott asked.

"A 30 percent volume increase is definitely positive for profit growth."

"How much incremental expense do you think we'll have to cover costs for commission, delivery, warehousing etc. for this order?" Wondering where the conversation was going, Jake offered an estimate of one thousand dollars.

"Okay, let's create a simple income statement showing the impact on profits before and after the change," Scott suggested. "We'll use actual costs for the cost of goods sold (COGS) line and calculate expenses at 26 percent of the total sale for the original order, since that was our expense-to-sales ratio last year. Then we'll add one thousand dollars to that figure for the expenses for the *after* scenario. If they're good business people, they'll pay five days earlier to get the extra 2 percent discount, so let's use a 7 percent discount in our calculations. Finally, we'll calculate percentage change on pre-tax income."

Jake didn't have a financial background and was unsure how to proceed, so Scott did most of the calculations as follows:

Background information before the volume increase:

- Sold 1000 cases @ $100 each = $100,000
- COGS 1000 cases @ $72 each = $72,000
- Expenses estimated @ $26,000 (26% of sales)

Background information after the 30% volume increase and 7% price discount:

- Sales estimated @ 1,300 cases @ $93 each = $120,900
- COGS 1,300 cases @ $72 each = $93,600
- Expenses estimated to increase by $1,000 to $27,000

Sunrise Grocery Business

	Before	After
Sales	$100,000	$120,900
Cost of Goods Sold	72,000	93,600
Gross Profit	28,000	27,300
Expenses	26,000	27,000
Pre Tax Income	$ 2,000	$ 300
% Change on Pre Tax Income	+ 0%	- 85%

Jake couldn't believe his eyes. What he thought was a profitable sale turned out to be a huge money loser! What a mistake!

"I'm sure your intentions were good, Jake," Scott continued, noticing Jake's embarrassment. "From the outside, it looked like a good deal. Don't worry—you're not the only rep who thought cutting price to get volume would make us more successful. Why do you think there's such a huge negative impact on the bottom line?"

"I guess it's a margin problem."

"Yes, we are a low margin, low return business, which means we don't earn much profit from a dollar in sales. Any price discount we give has a huge multiplier effect on the bottom line. The impact wouldn't be nearly as great if we were a high-margin business like many pharmaceutical and software businesses. Our second problem is that our expenses as a percentage of sales have been gradually increasing while our margins are compressing. That's a bad combination. Now that you've seen this, I'm sure you'll look at deals from a different perspective in the future."

Later that day, when Jake met with Steve at Hamptons, he learned that Scott had worked through a similar income statement exercise with Steve to assess the profitability of a sale. "I called on Sam Shaw at A-1 Janitorial," recounted Steve, "to introduce him to our new XL line of cleaning chemicals. Before I even got started, Sam mentioned he was thinking of canceling our agreement since he didn't see us adding value to his business. Unsure of what to do, I asked Sam what it would take to keep his business until I could get back to him with more details on how we've added value to his business. As usual, his response was, 'I need a price discount.' He also let it slip that he was using a competitor's cleaning chemicals on some of his jobs and was considering standardizing to that product. This came as a surprise to me and created an opportunity for us to increase our business—or, conversely, for the competitor to increase their business at our expense.

"After some negotiation Sam agreed to renew the order if we could lower his product costs by 5 percent for the next six months. Of course he wanted a price concession but I saw this as a perfect opportunity to introduce the new XL line. As you know, many of the products in the XL line contain more concentrated chemicals which effectively lower the users costs. At the same time, our cost is 5 percent lower than the other line, so it's a win/win deal. Sam eventually agreed to order about 5 percent fewer cases if I provided free training for his staff, which I'd get the manufacturer's rep to do. The sell price remains the same but we need to prove he can get the same job done using 5 percent less product. In some ways, I think he just wanted to feel like he had negotiated a good deal. I walked out relieved, knowing we had retained the business for another six months.

"When I met with Scott later that day," Steve went on, "he was very pleased and asked me what I thought the impact on profits would be. I answered, 'We're better off by 5 percent because of lower costs.' He responded by pulling out a piece of paper and walking me through the same exercise you did. Here are my notes:

Before

Sell 180 cases @ $100 per case	$ 18,000.00
COGS (180 cases @ $70 per case)	12,600.00
Gross Margin	5,400.00
Expenses @ 26% of sales	4,680.00
Pre Tax Income	$ 720.00

After (Sell the XL Line)

Sell 170 cases @ $100 per case	$ 17,000.00
COGS (170 @ $66.50 per case)	11,305.00
Gross Margin	5,695.00
Expenses @ 26% of sales	4,420.00
Pre Tax Income	$ 1,275.00
% Change on Pre Tax Income	+77.1%

"What I thought was only a 5 percent gain turned out to be 77 percent more profitable for BD!" Steve exclaimed. "I couldn't believe it at first."

Jake and Steve were both shocked that the result could turn out so differently from what they had expected. Turning to Jake, Steve asked, "How are we supposed to know all this stuff?"

"I don't know, I guess this is what Scott was referring to at Vic's when he said he can't be involved in every call we make, so the future of this company rests largely on our decision-making skills and our understanding of the profit drivers and profit leaks in our business."

At home later that evening, Jake hesitated as he went to pick up his laptop sitting by the front door. Having the latest road warrior tools had been exciting at first, but the novelty had long since worn off. It simply meant he could work anytime or anywhere and was always accessible. Work followed Jake wherever he went. His laptop traveled with the family on vacations; his phone could ring anytime of the day; emails arrived 24/7. Some customers and work associates even expected a response outside of normal working hours. The reality of having the latest technology had become part of his life. Jake felt trapped.

"Why don't you take a break tonight, honey?" Jess suggested, noticing his lack of energy and the tired look on his face. She knew he was feeling stressed as he tried to increase sales and make more money to offset increased expenses and the loss of her income.

Jess's suggestion was all it took to convince Jake that he needed a break. After tucking Michelle in bed, he decided to head out to the local bookstore on 49th, where he would grab a coffee, sit down, browse through a few books and relax. *No cell phone, no PDA, no laptop and no internet for me tonight—just a good old-fashioned book*, Jake thought.

He slowly backed his car out of the driveway and headed down the road. He had hardly put the big white sedan into gear when he noticed the new BMW in the Millers' driveway just ahead. He looked enviously at his dream car sitting in their driveway, perfectly polished as if it had just come from the dealer's showroom. He wished it were sitting in his driveway. Six or seven years younger than Jake, Ben Miller seemed to have made all the right decisions in life. Ben's business continued to grow rapidly and he seemed to have a knack for the stock market. Every few years, the Millers made a pile of money on real estate when they traded up for a larger house. What a contrast to the Wrights, who lived almost directly across the street from the Millers. They had a new Audi sitting in the driveway and a nice house, but that's where the similarities ended. They had borrowed money in the late '90s to buy tech stocks and lost most of it in the ensuing stock market meltdown, forcing them to take out a second mortgage on the house. Then Greg

Wright lost his job and was unemployed for six months. With no savings and high expenses, they struggled to make ends meet every month. Despite all the setbacks, though, they somehow managed to drive a new Audi.

As Jake turned the corner and entered the business district, he realized for the first time that if he knew the real story behind these businesses, he'd probably find the same extremes as he did on his own street with the Millers and the Wrights. Some businesses flourished while others struggled. Some seemed to be prospering, but their financials suggested otherwise. Others didn't look like much but were highly profitable. Some entrepreneurs and managers with no formal business training could run successful businesses, while others with degrees in business couldn't turn a profit no matter what they did. According to Jake's assessment, BD fell somewhere in the lower quartile.

It was dark outside when Jake arrived at the bookstore, but the interior of the store was bright and well lit. The store had created a comfortable, relaxed environment where people wanted to read. Jake couldn't remember the last time he had set foot in a bookstore. In fact, he hadn't read one book during the past year. Reading required leisure time, something he didn't have.

Jake proceeded down the main aisle, which was carpeted to muffle sound. At the front of the store were shelves full of magazines, followed by row upon row of books. The perimeter of the store was several feet higher, creating the appearance of levels, which made it easier to see displays that were further away. In the center of an aisle Jake came upon a large display filled with books on how to get rich. "With titles like *How to Become a Millionaire,* how could they *not* be bestsellers?" Jake muttered under his breath. It wasn't what he was looking for, but he picked up a copy and continued on to the Mystery section.

After choosing several novels, he found a comfortable leather chair and sank into it. Within thirty minutes, he had decided on a mystery novel, although *the millionaire* book had appeal. What had caught his interest was a compound interest table that showed how earning just 1 percent more on savings could result in a huge gain down the road. Saving one hundred dollars per month invested at 9 percent accumulated to about $468,000 after forty years, but saving the same amount invested at 10 percent accumulated to roughly $632,000 forty years later. In other words, the extra 1 percent resulted in about $164,000 more, or put another way, 35% more at retirement. For a guy in his early thirties who had barely begun saving for retirement, those looked like big numbers!

Jake's spirits lifted the following morning when he awoke to a bright, sunny day. While he was preparing to leave for work, he told Jess about the compound interest example he had read the night before. Although impressed by the outcome, Jess was more concerned about what she had to do that day and what bills were due at month-end rather than at retirement forty years later. As he was walking out the door, she asked, "Does that same 1 percent principle apply at work?"

"It probably would if we were a bank," Jake answered quickly, "but we're a distribution company. If anything, we borrow money and make the banks rich off that principal." Then he said goodbye and headed off to work, hoping to beat the rush hour.

In early April the envelope containing March results appeared on Scott's desk just like it had previously for Kirk. Unlike Kirk, Scott had time to turn things around. It was too soon to have made a difference, but Scott didn't want to waste time. As he leaned back in his chair, he mulled over his options. It had become apparent to him that Jake and Steve did not understand the multiplier effect of their daily decisions even though they were two of the better performers. He concluded that the balance of the reps and office staff likely were unaware of the impact they had as well. One option was to make some personnel changes, but that would be his last resort. A second option was to shake things up by changing roles and territories, but that would take time, ruffle a lot of feathers and impact customers. After further thought, he decided to fast-track the training he had in mind and hope the employees would become fully engaged in finding 1 percent improvements. If he could accomplish that, the results would come. Within a few minutes, he had contacted the trainer he had used in the past, booked a date and written an e-mail to the sales team, inviting them to a half-day meeting in a couple of weeks. The rest of the employees would complete the training two weeks after the reps.

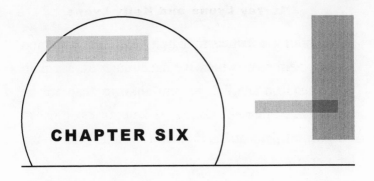

CHAPTER SIX

In the weeks following the dinner at Vic's, morale in the office improved. Before Scott's arrival, hope and encouragement had vanished, replaced by worry and concern. Employees lamented about how the world had changed, how bad things were and the only way to compete was on price. They focused on the barriers to success. Scott, on the other hand, focused on the keys to success. Under Scott's management, a renewed sense of hope returned to the employees. Everybody was energized. They felt as if they were off to a fresh start with a leader who believed in them.

Early one morning, during a meeting with Scott, Caroline Edwards asked him how things were going.

"Fine, so far," Scott answered. "It seems like a great team here. I haven't detected any serious issues. All I have to do now is generate results."

"Results would be nice. That's why we hired you. Tell me, what changes are you planning?"

"Nothing significant. Big changes take time and money, neither of which we have much of. My plan is to focus on small 1 percent changes that can be implemented immediately."

"Only 1 percent!" exclaimed Caroline. "We need a lot more than that."

"Don't worry. One percent in key areas will get you a lot more than you think."

"I'd like to see that. How do you plan to tell them?"

"I don't plan to tell them."

"If you don't tell them, who will?"

"Nobody is going to tell them," Scott explained, "because adults don't learn well when they're told what to do. The reps have been told countless times not to cut prices, but they still do it. The staff was asked to cut expenses last year, but, in fact, expenses rose. The traditional approach is to tell people what to do because it's fast and easy, but I believe people learn best through experience and discovery. I plan to help them discover the key principles that drive profit and loss in our business."

"How do you plan to do that?"

"I hired a trainer I've used in the past to run a business simulation that deals with the same business issues and decisions we face every day. By the end of the simulation they'll clearly understand the big picture and the importance of growing sales and improving profitability. They'll also learn the key financial and business skills critical to running a distribution business."

"What happens after that?" Caroline asked.

"I'll tie those concepts to our business using our financials and real examples. They'll figure out the real profit drivers and their role in producing profits."

"Couldn't you avoid the expense by just doing the exercise and forgetting the simulation?"

"I could, but most employees don't understand finance and no one has ever taken the time to explain it to them. Flashing up slide after slide of income statements and ratios will put people to sleep. Having them run a business like ours and make decisions will be fun, energizing and, of course, challenging."

"Sounds interesting. Let me know how it goes."

Not much changed over the next week—although Jake was impressed when Scott took the two employees who hadn't been able to attend the dinner at Vic's out to lunch. Scott left nothing to chance and made a point of getting people involved in the business. As time passed, employees became better acquainted with the new branch manager and more comfortable in his presence. Familiarity gradually replaced fear of the unknown. In time, even the skeptical employees began to believe in Scott's approach. Scott was different from any other manager Jake had worked with in the past, so he decided to study Scott and his leadership style.

The invitation from Scott to all branch staff finally arrived. It read, "Please plan to attend a business simulation training program on the afternoon of April 15 from 12:30 PM to 4:30 PM at the Holiday Inn." Scott invited all the employees, although attendance was optional for the drivers. Other than limited computer training, BD hadn't invested much in employee training, so everybody perceived the business simulation as a perk.

April 15 was overcast, but the room at the Holiday Inn was bright and spacious. Those who arrived early looked curiously at the game boards, casino style chips and other materials lying on each table. It looked interesting—not the typical lecture format, that was for sure. Scott understood people well and seldom gave them answers; he encouraged them to discover the answers on their own.

After everyone was seated, Scott said warmly, "Welcome to our first training session. Regardless of how much experience you may have, I've always believed in learning. This is the first session of many I hope to implement over the next couple of years. A few weeks ago at Vic's, I mentioned that you are all business people and that your daily decisions—ones I don't have time to be involved in—affect profitability. So, today you're going to experience how businesses like ours work financially and operationally. You'll run a business, experience the results and learn business and financial skills. In the coming weeks, we'll hold two follow up sessions, where we'll build on these skills and discover how small changes impact BD's financial results. By the way, there will be a prize for the team that generates the best results."

A prize! Now he had everybody's attention!

"Now let me turn this session over to our facilitator—David Redding."

"Thank you and welcome," David began. "This afternoon, you're going to have fun running a business. We've placed you in teams of four, each team member having a specific role. Your task is to turn this business around. Your specific objectives are to:

1. Increase sales
2. Increase profits
3. Turn inventory more quickly
4. Collect money from your customers a little faster
5. Reduce debt

"Does any of this sound familiar?" Scott piped up. Everyone laughed, knowing this was exactly what BD needed to do.

"There are several strategies that you can implement in the simulation," David explained. "For example, you can change your selling price. If you reduce price, we'll reward you with extra volume. On the other hand, if you increase your price, we'll assume you lose some business to lower-priced competitors like that online distributor down in Portland. You may invest in sales to grow the business or make operational investments to decrease your operating expenses, as you did with the new inventory system you implemented last year. All strategies can work, although some work better than others. Although each of you has specific roles, you'll do better if you work together as a team, just like at BD. You'll have three years to reach the objectives. We'll stop at the end of each year to assess your performance with an income statement and key ratios, just like at BD." After a few more instructions, the teams began working the simulation.

At the end of year one of the simulation, results were mixed—some teams lost money while others made money. One team that lost money was perplexed by the fact that they generated cash but no profit. At the end of year two, a wide variation in results between the teams emerged. The "Profits R Us" team was in the lead and things were getting very competitive. This didn't feel like a typical training course—each team was very much engaged, and it was fun and relevant. Nobody wanted to take a break. By the end of year three, a new winner had emerged. "Profits R Us" had made a strategic error by lowering their price. They had a big sales increase, but profits plummeted. The "Doctor Profit" team emerged victorious. David Redding had done a superb job of relating the strategies and tactics the teams used in the game to the decisions BD employees made every day.

At the end of the session, David asked the teams what they had learned about running a business. Responses included:

1. It was very difficult to meet the profit goal when we lowered price. We didn't realize cutting price had such a negative impact on the bottom line;

2. If we built up inventory and the sales didn't materialize, it forced us to borrow money. This increased our interest expense and decreased our profits. Carrying excess inventory was costly;

3. If we didn't do a good job collecting outstanding receivables, it forced us to borrow money to operate the business. This increased

our interest expense, which decreased our profits;

4. In a low-margin business, you need to operate very efficiently. There's little room for error;

5. If you can find a way to justify a higher price and not lose much volume, this strategy can be very profitable.

Employees had already begun to see the connection between what happened in the simulation and what was happening every day at BD. After all, BD had low turns, took a long time to collect receivables (higher than average Day Sales Outstanding), and they regularly cut price to make a sale.

The review continued for another ten minutes. Then Scott walked to the front of the room and asked the group, "What's the purpose of a business?"

The responses came quickly: to serve customers, to provide great quality at reasonable prices, to create value, and to make money.

"That's the answer I'm looking for!" exclaimed Scott. "We're in business to *make money*. Exceeding customer expectations and providing great service is part of our strategy and it's necessary just to be competitive, but at the end of the day, we're here to make money. Money is the measuring stick of business. It's our primary goal.

I want you to remember that. Over the coming weeks, we'll complete Part Two of the training course where we'll examine how decisions similar to the ones you made today translate into profit or loss at BD. Regardless of what department you work in, you affect financial performance. Obviously, we need you to understand how you create financial value for BD."

It was late in the day and late in the week, but Jake didn't feel tired. On the contrary, the business simulation exercise had energized him and provided clarity on how to make a business successful, something he planned to do in his career. Ideas were flooding his head as he drove home. He didn't need Part Two to see how some of the decisions he made every day were negatively impacting BD.

When Jake arrived home, Jess announced that the Millers would be coming over for coffee the next evening. Their neighbors, the Millers, were good friends and Jake always enjoyed their company.

The Miller's arrived shortly after eight o'clock on Saturday night. The conversation flowed easily from subject to subject until the women got into decorating ideas. At that point, Ben Miller and Jake began talking about typical "guy" subjects like sports and business. Ben ran a successful business, so Jake told him about the simulation in which he had participated and how his manager planned to show them how even a small 1 percent change can have a huge impact on profitability.

"The simulation sounds very interesting," Ben said. "The concept of 1 percent changes fascinates me. I've always known about the importance of 1 percent changes in the world of investments, but I never thought about how this concept might also apply to my business. I'll have to spend some time thinking that one through."

Curious, Jake asked, "How do you apply it to investing?"

"One principle that many investment professionals adhere to is that success has more to do with *time in the market* than *timing the market*. For example, last year the S&P 500 Index rose 3 percent, but if you took out the top two trading days (about 1 percent of trading days), the index would have been flat. In other words, you would've lost 100 percent of your profit if you owned the index through an exchange-traded fund and weren't invested for those two days."

"Wow! A year of profits gone in two days!"

"Yes," Ben continued. "The second is the age-old principle of compound interest, which you'll find in almost every personal finance book ever published. I've always been amazed at the wealth you can build over time using this principle and how a mere 1 percent change in your rate of return can make a difference of several hundred thousand dollars at retirement. The example I share with people is, if you invest $200 per month at 10% from age twenty to age sixty-five, you'll end up with about $1.8 million dollars at age sixty-five. However, if you invested the same $200 per month over the same time period and earned 11% compounded interest, you'd have about $2.5 million at age sixty-five. In this case, an 11% versus a 10% return means an extra $700,000 in your pocket."

"That's great, but who can save $200 per month?" Jake lamented.

"Not everyone, but most people could save more than they do now. As I see it, the bigger problem is you have to wait decades for the result and most people don't want to wait. We want a new TV today, a new car next year . . . the list goes on. Before you know it, you're middle-aged, and by the time you realize how far behind you are in saving for retirement, you don't have enough time to catch up. You finally get to the point where you can start to save money and then something else comes along, like college for the kids. It's a never-ending cycle. People need to change their approach to managing money . . . but we'll save that conversation for another day."

Ben's passionate and confident comments about saving for retirement inspired Jake to think through his own retirement savings plan. The reality was that Jake was saving much less than $200 per month and he didn't even know his rate of return. Jake wanted to ask Ben more questions but felt the timing wasn't right. Before he knew it, it was midnight and the Millers were walking out the door.

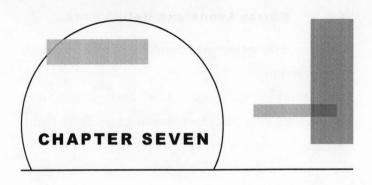

CHAPTER SEVEN

Part two of the training for the reps took place on a Friday afternoon in mid-May. As Scott advanced through his slides, it was apparent that first-quarter profit had changed little compared to the same period last year. Sales remained flat, margins had not improved and expenses as a percentage of sales were still too high. They were obviously behind plan. With less than eight months left in the year, meeting targets seemed unachievable.

Scott stated clearly that they had a problem, but at the same time was confident they would start to turn the corner in the current quarter.

"What can we do differently to turn things around?" Steve asked.

"Effective immediately, we will search for 1 percent improvements," Scott replied.

"But we're behind plan. Surely we need a lot more than 1 percent."

"In areas like sales we do, but all I'm looking for now are 1 percent changes. Does anyone in the room think they cannot improve by 1 percent?"

No hands went up. Compared to the stretch goals Kirk had asked for, finding 1 percent seemed easy.

"Okay, let's get started then. First of all, as sales reps, what decisions do you make everyday that impact our financial results?"

Their responses included decisions that directly or indirectly relate to:

- sales volume;
- pricing and margin;
- improve sales/product mix;

"That's a good list," Scott said. "The first thing you need to know is that through these decisions, you impact the financial health of this company more than any other employee group because the decisions you make affect the biggest line on our income statement—the sales line. To illustrate how critical your decisions are, let's look at our income statement. My first example has to do with sell price.

"What do you think happens to pre-tax income if we reduce sell price by just 1 percent on every order?"

The reps thought pre-tax income would drop 1%-25%.

"If we reduce sell price by 1 percent on the same volume, will our COGS decrease?" Karen responded that COGS would not decrease.

"Will our expenses decrease?"

"Most expenses will remain the same," Steve volunteered, "except for commission, which should drop slightly."

"I agree, Steve," Scott said, "so I've reduced expenses by $45,000 and kept COGS the same. Let's take a look at the results."

Lower Sell Price 1%

	Before	After
Sales	$29,700,000	$29,403,000
Cost of Goods Sold	21,600,000	21,600,000
Gross Profit	8,100,000	7,803,000
Expenses	7,722,000	7,677,000
Pre Tax Income	$ 378,000	$ 126,000
% Change on Pre Tax Income	+ 0%	- 67%

The reps were silent as the impact of the reduction in sell price sank in. Jake looked around the table. Obviously, no one had any idea that a mere 1 percent price decrease on every order would reduce pre-tax income by 67 percent.

Scott broke the silence. "Fortunately, the reverse is also true so a 1 percent price increase improves pre-tax income by 67 percent. Now, let's compare the pricing example with volume. If we increase volume by 1 percent, what other lines on the income statement will be affected?"

"COGS will go up by 1 percent and there will be some incremental commission to pay," Sue answered.

"What about other expenses?" Scott asked. "Do you think we could handle 1 percent more volume without taking up other expenses?"

"Yes," Sue responded.

"I agree," Scott said, "since this is only a volume improvement I have taken expenses up by $12,000. Had it been a margin improvement I would have taken expenses up more to account for increased commission paid on higher margin orders. Here's the result:

Increase Volume 1%

	Before	After
Sales	$29,700,000	$29,997,000
Cost of Goods Sold	21,600,000	21,816,000
Gross Profit	8,100,000	8,181,000
Expenses	7,722,000	7,734,000
Pre Tax Income	$ 378,000	$ 447,000
% Change on Pre Tax Income	+ 0%	+ 18.3%

"That's a great number, but if you had to choose between a 1 percent price increase versus a 1 percent volume increase, what would you choose?" Scott queried the group.

The reps all agreed that a price increase was much better than a volume increase.

"That's right," Scott said. "In fact, a 1 percent price increase has almost four times more impact to the bottom line than a 1 percent volume increase. We know this because if you multiply 18.3 by four, it's almost the same as the 67 percent we get from a 1 percent price increase. So, my question to you is: what can you do to increase our average selling price?"

At this point, Scott met with some resistance. Donna Becker, who had a reputation for discounting price, argued, "That's fine on paper, but it's very competitive out there. You want us to increase sales, but if we don't discount, we'll lose business."

"Your point is well taken, Donna. Let's postpone the discussion on increasing price for now and focus on discounting. I ran a report recently that showed that only 20 percent of our sales are at full price, which means we discount 80 percent of the time. What increments do you use when you're offering a price discount?"

Donna replied, "I usually negotiate in 5 percent increments. I offer anywhere from 5%-15%, depending on who I'm competing with and the starting margin."

"How about everyone else? Do you think in 5 percent increments?" Scott asked.

Most of the reps said they did, although some negotiated in 10 percent increments. Unlike the others, though, Sue Ho was at the other end of the scale—she negotiated in 2 percent increments. Sue's strategy piqued everyone's interest; everyone knew she had generated the most gross profit dollars last year after receiving the famous white envelope. Her results had earned her the respect of the other reps.

"Why do you negotiate in 2 percent increments, Sue?" Scott enquired.

"Because everyone asks for more than they want and I don't want to leave money on the table. I often win new business with a smaller discount than I think I'll need. That's one of the ways I keep margins up."

Scott posed another question to the group. "When you discount price, how much more volume do you need to generate the same gross profit dollars?"

A sea of blank looks met his gaze. Frankly, no one knew how to answer this question—nobody had ever asked it before.

"Managers, senior executives and owners never want to see fewer gross profit dollars (GP$) flowing into the business," Scott continued. "They want to see more GP$ flowing in. You can offset a price reduction with additional volume, but most reps, managers, senior executives and owners would be shocked to learn how much more volume they need. Let me illustrate with the following example:

- Assume you sell one case of product to a customer
- Selling price is $100 per case
- Cost is $80 per case
- You decide to reduce the sell price by 10% to $90

To determine how much additional volume you need, complete the following steps:

Step 1:   Determine gross profit dollars (GP$) generated for the order before and after the price change.

Step 2: Use the following formula to determine how much additional volume you must sell to generate the same gross profit dollars:

Using the above scenario, we calculate the additional volume required as follows:

$$\frac{\text{(Old GP\$ - New GP\$)}}{\text{New GP\$}} \times 100 = \% \text{ Additional Volume}$$

	Sell Price	Cost	Gross Profit
GP $ Before Price Reduction	$100	$80	$20
GP $ After Price Reduction	$90	$80	$10

$$\frac{\$20 \text{ (Old GP\$) - \$10 (New GP\$)}}{\$10 \text{ (New GP\$)}} \times 100 = 100\%$$

"That's right. You would require 100% additional volume to generate the same gross profit dollars. Everyone was shocked by the answer. My second question is: what happens to expenses if volume increases 100%?"

"They would skyrocket," Jake answered.

"Yes," Scott responded. "Unless the volume increase could be offset by a lower cost of goods sold, assuming you can negotiate lower costs. However, the bottom line is that you need a significant volume increase—especially in a low-margin business—to offset a price reduction."

Scott posed another question to the sales reps. "Does a good negotiator start by asking for more than they want?" All of them agreed this was a basic negotiating tactic. "But if you hear the words 'we need a lower price' over and over, are you likely to start believing it yourself?"

Most of the reps nodded.

"And do you buy the lowest-priced clothes, cars, housing and food for you and your family?"

"Of course not!" the reps exclaimed in unison.

"I'm sure you would like lower prices but you're also willing to pay more for quality, service, convenience and many other factors. Our customers are not much different. Of course they want to pay less and it's their responsibility to ask but they will pay for value just like you. Pricing issues can be just as much a psychological barrier for you as they are a practical barrier for our customers. We need to start believing in ourselves and start convincing customers that our prices are fair and reasonable. We simply can't afford to discount 80 percent of the time.

"Let's move on to my final example," Scott continued, "which has to do with sales mix. As you know, we have thousands of products that we sell at various margin levels ranging from 15% to 50%. Depending on who's selling and the volumes involved, even the same products are sold at different margin levels. Our average margin for the branch is 27.3%. I arrived at this number by dividing our gross profit of $8,100,000 into sales of $29,700,000. Now, let's see what happens when we change our sales mix to sell slightly higher volumes of high-margin value added products like our XL line and slightly lower volumes of commodity like low-margin products.

"To illustrate, I've assumed that 63.6% of our sales fall into the commodity category averaging 20% margin and the balance of sales are value added products averaging 40% margin. For the 'after' scenario, I assumed that 60% of sales are commodity and 40% of sales come from higher margin value added products. Finally, I assumed we lost almost 6% of our commodity business, but grew our value added products by 10%. Note that the overall sales line does not change at all. We know this is doable because other BD branches have a better mix than we have in Seattle. What follows is a table showing the sales mix change followed by an income statement showing the impact on the bottom

Before Sales Mix Change

	Sales ($)	Margin (%)	Margin ($)
Commodity	$ 18,900,000	20%	$ 3,780,000
Value Add	$ 10,800,000	40%	$ 4,320,000
Total	$ 29,700,000	27.3%	$ 8,100,000

After Sales Mix Change

	Sales ($)	Margin (%)	Margin ($)
Commodity	$ 17,820,000	20%	$ 3,564,000
Value Add	$ 11,880,000	40%	$ 4,752,000
Total	$ 29,700,000	28%	$ 8,316,000

line. Note that I have increased expenses by $30,000 to cover increased commission paid on higher margin products."

Income Statement With Sales Mix Change

	Before	After
Sales	$29,700,000	$29,700,000
Cost of Goods Sold	21,600,000	21,384,000
Gross Profit	8,100,000	8,316,000
Expenses	7,722,000	7,752,000
Pre Tax Income	$ 378,000	$ 564,000
% Change on Pre Tax Income	+ 0%	+ 49.2%

The result was unbelievable! On the one hand, this was more than a 1 percent shift in sales mix. On the other hand, the reps knew it was achievable. The reps had discussed selling more high-margin products at sales meetings, but had never implemented the idea. From a sales perspective, they thought it was easier and took less time to maintain the current business. They thought they could invest the extra time in generating new sales but the problem was they never did and Kirk had never shown them the financial impact of selling higher-margin products.

"Steve had an interesting example a couple weeks ago," Scott went on, "where he was selling the XL line to A1 Janitorial. I asked him to complete an income statement on that piece of business. Steve, why don't you give us a brief rundown on what happened and how it impacted pre-tax."

"First of all," Steve began, "the customer was considering canceling his account with us because he felt we weren't adding enough value to his business. I proposed he try out our XL line to lower his costs, as 5 percent less product would do the same job due to the more concentrated chemicals. I also offered free training on how to use the products correctly which I plan to get the manufacturer's rep to do. In the end I managed to maintain the same sell price per case but sold roughly 5 percent fewer cases. When Scott asked me about the impact on profitability, I assumed we were ahead by 5 percent because of the XL line's lower costs. However, after running the numbers, I discovered the pre-tax income for this order increased by 77 percent!"

"That's a real life example of the power of selling higher margin products," Scott said. "Let me show you another way of looking at this principle," Scott said, putting up another slide.

	Product A	Product B
Gross Profit % to Sales	27%	31%
Expenses as a % of Sales	26%	26%
Return on Sales	1%	5%

"Before looking at the comparison, I'd like to make some comments about the "Expenses as a Percent of Sales" line. Businesses have both fixed and variable costs. Fixed costs like rent, vehicle lease costs, insurance and even a large portion of our payroll costs, do not change with volume and remain relatively fixed month after month. On the other hand, variable expenses like overtime and commission change with volume. For the most part, the majority of our expenses are fixed and the table assumes this.

"Now, when you look at the table what do you see? Is Product B four percent more profitable than Product A (31% gross profit compared to 27% gross profit), or is it five times more profitable (5% ROS vs. 1% ROS)?"

Almost everyone agreed it was five times more profitable. In the past, BD management had told the reps to push high-margin products. Sometimes they complied and sometimes they didn't. Without understanding the financial impact of their actions, they usually did what was easiest. With knowledge like this, the reps began to feel more like business people who understood the impact of their decisions.

Then Donna posed an interesting question to Scott. "Isn't *any* order better than no order?"

"Let me direct that question back to the group. Under what circumstances might any order be better than no order?"

The group's responses included:

- We need volume to hit a sales target;
- We need volume to cover fixed costs;
- It gets us in the door to sell higher margin products;
- The extra volume helps us earn rebates from our suppliers;
- Large order size (covers average cost per order);
- It increases our market share.

"Now let me ask the more difficult part of the question," Scott said. "Under what conditions might it be better to lose the order?"

The reps offered several answers, including:

- When a lower price becomes a new benchmark for the customer or worse yet for the market;
- There is no profit in the order;
- Small order size (does not cover average cost per order);
- The customer is high maintenance and it's not worth the effort.

"I guess you've answered the question," Scott stated. "Sometimes it makes sense and sometimes it doesn't. Our goal is to improve profitability—that's why we're in business. If we continue to chase orders based on price, we won't improve the profitability of our business."

"So we need to increase our markup by 5 percent?" Donna piped up.

"No, we need to increase our *margin* by five percent. There's a big difference between *markup* and *margin*," Scott explained patiently. "*Markup* is based on cost while *margin* is based on sell price. For example, if you have a cost of $5 and a sell price of $10, you have $5 of gross profit or margin. This is the equivalent of 100% markup ($5 of gross profit divided by a $5 cost). However, the margin is only 50 percent—$5 of gross profit divided by the $10 sell price. Therefore, a 100% markup is the equivalent of 50% margin."

Trying to defend her position, Donna asked another tough question. "Are you prepared to lose business if we increase our prices?"

"I expect we'll lose some business, but it's your job to minimize that by justifying the price and adding value to the customer. Tell me, Donna, if you increased sell price on average by 5 percent, how much volume do you think you might lose?"

"I wouldn't be surprised if I lost 10 percent of my volume."

"Okay, let's assume your cost is $75 per case, your average margin is 25 percent and you sell ten cases at $100 each."

Before Price Increase

Sell 10 cases @ $100	$1000
COGS 10 cases @ $75	750
Gross Margin $	$ 250
Gross Margin % ($250 / $1,000)	25%

After Price Increase

Sell 9 cases @ $105	$945
COGS 9 cases @ $75	675
Gross Margin $	$ 270
Gross Margin % ($270 / $945)	28.6%

"As you can see," Scott pointed out, "you're still ahead in GM$ even after losing 10 percent of your volume. In fact, GM% has improved from 25% to 28.6%! All I ask of you and the others is that you think about the impact of price increases and decreases, keeping in mind our goal of increasing profitability."

After further discussion, Scott closed the meeting. "I'll be meeting with the rest of the office staff on May 22, next Friday afternoon. We'll be focusing on 1 percent changes and how they apply to expenses, COGS and asset management. I'd like all of you to attend the meeting so that everyone sees the same examples and has a common understanding of the financial impacts."

The reps dispersed, feeling empowered and invigorated. This sales meeting was different from any other they had attended. They had learned to look at their business from a new perspective and been challenged to find a way to improve their results by 1 percent.

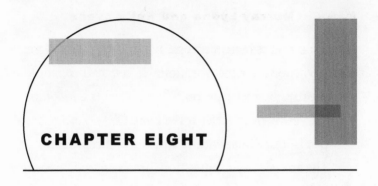

CHAPTER EIGHT

As the days grew longer and warmer, it began to feel more like summer and less like spring. The ocean breeze was cool, yet comfortable. Basketball season was winding down and baseball was in high gear. On a bright, sunny day in late May, all the branch employees assembled for the last module of Scott's training session.

Scott began the meeting by thanking everyone for attending. "As you know, we held a follow-up session with the sales group last week, so you might be wondering why they're here today."

"Because they're slow learners," Jim from Purchasing quipped.

Everybody except the reps laughed.

"Not exactly," Scott replied. "That session focused on sales opportunities. Today, we'll look at branch-wide opportunities. First, I want to review the sales slides I showed last week and then we'll move on to the scenarios that affect everyone in the branch. Let me begin with one simple question: If you had to, could you improve by just 1 percent?"

Everybody nodded in agreement.

"But is it worth spending time on?" Jim asked.

"The answer to your question, Jim, is an unequivocal *yes*," replied Scott. "In fact, it makes a far more significant difference than most people think. I'll give you some examples in a few minutes, but first I have one more question: In each of the areas represented here today, how do your decisions impact profitability?"

Scott summarized their answers on a flipchart:

- Sales and Customer Service reps affect sales, volume and sales mix;
- Buyers affect cost of goods sold (COGS) and inventory turns;
- Virtually everyone affects expenses;
- Credit and Collections affect DSO, who qualifies for terms and sometimes the acceptance of new customers if they present a credit risk;
- Drivers and warehouse employees primarily affect delivery expenses and some warehousing expenses, excluding rent.

"As you can see," Scott said, "everyone here affects one or more areas on our income statement. What I'm going to do is show you the impact and then we'll talk about simple ways you can have a positive impact in the near future. Let's begin by reviewing the scenarios Sales and Customer Service reps influence the most."

Scott put up the price, volume increase and sales mix slides he had shown the reps one week earlier. Again, there was dead silence. Everyone was astonished by the effect of such a small change.

"Now you know the difference 1 percent makes in the sales area, let's look at the difference it makes to the areas you influence? Let's begin by reducing COGS, which is the primary responsibility of buyers." Scott brought up the next slide.

Decrease COGS 1%

	Before	After
Sales	$29,700,000	$29,700,000
Cost of Goods Sold	21,600,000	21,384,000
Gross Profit	8,100,000	8,316,000
Expenses	7,722,000	7,722,000
Pre Tax Income	$ 378,000	$ 594,000
% Change on Pre Tax Income	+ 0%	+ 57.1%

"As you can see, by finding 1 percent those of you in Purchasing can improve branch profitability by 57 percent. The flip side of this is if our costs went up 1 percent and the sales reps weren't able to pass those increases along, then it would negatively impact the bottom line by 57 percent, so Sales and Customer Service reps also need to be aware of this. Now, what are some of the ways you can reduce COGS?"

The group's responses included:
- Negotiate lower prices;
- Negotiate terms so BD gets a discount for paying early;
- Ask for volume discounts;
- Ask for more than you want from the supplier;
- Ask for incentives like free product if BD hits certain targets;
- Negotiate rebates;
- Reduce the number of suppliers and then negotiate volume discounts;

"We'll come back to these ideas, but first let's look at something everyone here impacts—managing expenses. Jake, imagine you've just returned home after being on the road for several days and your travel expenses total $500. Could you have done the same trip for $495?"

Jake concurred it would be easy to save five bucks.

"Jim," Scott continued, "you recently ordered a new laptop. How much did it cost?"

"Twelve hundred dollars," Jim replied.

"Could you have saved $12 on that purchase?"

"I guess so."

"And finally," Scott added, "let's assume collectively we spent $3,000 on office supplies last month. If we all tried to conserve a little, do you think we could have got by on $30 less?"

Everyone agreed it would be easy. This was the equivalent of one small courier bill. "These examples all represent 1 percent changes. So, let's see what happens if we had reduced last year's branch expenses by 1 percent."

Reduce Expenses 1%

	Before	After
Sales	$29,700,000	$29,700,000
Cost of Goods Sold	21,600,000	21,600,000
Gross Profit	8,100,000	8,100,000
Expenses	7,722,000	7,644,780
Pre Tax Income	$ 378,000	$ 455,220
% Change on Pre Tax Income	+ 0%	+ 20.4%

Even though fixed expenses like rent couldn't easily be reduced, everyone believed the 1 percent expense reduction was feasible.

"I'm not advocating we spend all our time and energy on reducing expenses," Scott said. "Sometimes it makes more sense to spend money; however, one of our problems is that our expense-to-sales ratio is too high. In the simulation you discovered that low-margin businesses must be very efficient in order to be competitive. If you look at last year's expenses as a percentage of sales, they were 26 percent, which means that we have twenty-six cents of expenses for every dollar of sales. We need to get it down in the range of twenty-one cents for every dollar of sales so we can be more competitive with low cost providers.

"Over time, our margins have been squeezed while our expense-to-sales ratio has been rising. We're now at the point where the business isn't viable at current margin and expense levels. Let me illustrate this another way . . . how many dollars in sales must we generate to pay for one dollar in expenses if our margins average 27 percent?"

"Three dollars," Jim answered.

"In fact, it's a little more than that, Jim, since $3 multiplied by 27% equals $.81. The correct answer is $3.70. Here's a real example of how an avoidable expense affected our business just a few weeks ago: Because of a communication error, we had to rent a projector for $300 instead of using our own. To cover this expense at current margin levels, we have to generate sales of $1,111. Now think about how much extra effort is required to find new business totaling $1,111. The bottom line is that we need to be much more diligent around managing and reducing expenses."

Once again, silence descended upon the room. Everybody knew BD incurred avoidable expenses, but no one really seemed to care, and no one had ever communicated how much more revenue was required to cover those expenses. The good news was that most of the employees believed it wouldn't be difficult to find 1 percent.

Scott's next two examples showed how BD managed current assets. Putting up a slide showing BD's balance sheet, he asked, "What are the two biggest current assets in our business?"

The answer was obvious—Inventory and Accounts Receivable.

"Okay, let's begin by looking at inventory," Scott said. "In our industry, there are usually walls between Purchasing, Sales and the warehouse. Sales doesn't know exactly what they're going to sell in the next couple of months, so how is Purchasing supposed to know what to order? Sure, they have reference points like historical sales information, but it's still difficult to forecast the future. If Sales had their way, they would order large quantities of product so BD would never have to short-ship a customer. The benefit would be 100 percent fill rates; the downside is we would need to build another warehouse to store the extra product we would have to carry. Our cost for carrying the inventory would skyrocket and inventory turns would drop, which is the exact opposite of our goal.

"As you know, "inventory turns" refer to how many times we completely turn over our inventory in a year. Last year we averaged five turns, which was well below our target of six. In our industry, some businesses turn over their inventory eight or nine times per year, which is significantly better than our performance. With our new computer system in place, we should be able to improve inventory management this year. When inventory turns are low, more of our money is tied up in inventory and we need extra warehouse space to store, manage and handle it. We also have to carry extra insurance, which further increases our expenses.

"During the simulation, some of you discovered that when you had too much money tied up in inventory, you often ran short of cash when paying your suppliers and ongoing operating expenses. To continue operating, you had to borrow money from the bank, which increased your interest expense and decreased profitability. At BD, we have a bank loan to help finance inventory. To give you an idea of what this means to us financially, I've done a rough calculation showing our average investment in inventory. If we take our COGS line and divide it by the number of turns, we can find out our average inventory value."

COGS		Turns	Cash Tied Up
$21,600,000	÷	5	$4,320,000
$21,600,000	÷	7	$3,085,714
			$ 1,234,286

"As you can see, by improving turns from five to seven and maintaining that improvement, we can free up over one million dollars. However, if our turns drop back to five, we lose the financial benefit. My next question is: in our business who affects this metric?" The group concluded that Sales and Purchasing had the biggest impact but that other departments indirectly affected it as well.

"Okay, let's put inventory aside for a few minutes," Scott suggested, "and move on to our second biggest current asset—Accounts Receivable. When we're slow in collecting, we become a bank for our customers. Customers often buy and resell (or consume) our product before we are paid, which means we are still financing inventory long after it leaves the warehouse. Sales reps and employees in Credit and Collections influence this number the most. Let's look at the financial impact of slow collection.

"This calculation is simplified, but it gets the point across. All I'm doing is taking our annual sales and multiplying it by the number of day sales outstanding divided by 365. The result is a rough estimate of the amount of cash we have tied up in Receivables. In this

Sales		DSO	Cash Tied Up
$29,700,000	x	49 / 365	$3,987,123
$29,700,000	x	44 / 365	$3,580,274
			$ 406,849

example, I've compared our current DSO number of forty-nine with our goal of forty-four days.

"As you can see," Scott said, "we can potentially free up over $400,000 by collecting five days sooner. Even if we improved by only half that, we still free up $200,000.

Between inventory turns and DSO, we can potentially free up $1.6 million and reduce debt by this amount. We would save roughly $96,000 in interest expense at 6%. That alone is enough to improve our profitability by over 25 percent . . . and we haven't sold any more product, improved margins or reduced any of our operating expenses. That's why your help in managing assets is so critical!

"Of course," Scott continued, "we don't have complete control over when the customer pays us, but there are things we can do to help ensure payment occurs faster. For example, our invoices need to be error-free; by the time an error is corrected, it can easily add fifteen days to collection time. Secondly, we need to process our paperwork quickly and send out invoices as soon as possible so we don't add to the delay."

Once more, a hush descended upon the room, as employees realized for the first time how decisions related to invoicing and billing impacted financial performance.

"Now, it's time to find those opportunities," Scott declared. "I want you to generate ideas on how to find 1 percent differences."

Employees from Purchasing worked together to determine ways to reduce COGS and improve turns. Sales and Customer Service people worked on margin, mix and volume ideas. The remaining employees identified areas where they could reduce expenses or DSO. After twenty minutes, each group had prioritized their ideas on the flipcharts.

Scott began to work through the ideas from Purchasing first. No sooner had they begun discussing the first idea of reducing the number of suppliers when several sales reps protested, "We can't do that! When you eliminate a supplier, you might also lose a customer who wants those products." After a somewhat heated discussion, everybody agreed that although the idea had promise, it would take more work.

Amazingly, several of the buyers believed they could immediately find a 1 percent reduction in costs with some suppliers. When Scott asked why they hadn't done this in the past, they replied, "We didn't realize it was that big of a deal."

Some of the ideas were remarkably simple and easy to implement, while others required more work. Scott instructed everyone to select an idea they could implement easily within the next two weeks.

The ideas continued to flow when Scott moved on to expenses and DSO. He shared with the group an example of how his former employer had reduced DSO by seven days—largely by getting invoices out faster and reducing the number of errors on invoices. BD's own experience showed that when an error occurred on an invoice, the customer mailed the invoice back without paying until BD had investigated and corrected the problem. This easily added an extra fifteen days to the collection time.

Employees identified other ways to reduce simple expenses such as courier and office expenses. In the past, BD had focused more on growing sales and less on reducing expenses, so perhaps they had taken their eyes off the ball a little too much. Jake figured he could reduce his travel expenses by 10 percent through better planning.

Within thirty minutes, everyone in the room had developed a simple action item pertaining to some aspect of their job to work on in the next week. Because these action items didn't require meetings, approvals or reports, the employees could implement them immediately. Scott encouraged all employees to set a goal to reduce expenses by 2 percent by year-end.

Scot had one final slide.

"My last slide shows what happens when everyone on the team does their part to:
- Increase sell price by 1 percent;
- Increase volume by 1 percent;
- Change the sales mix;
- Decrease expenses by 1 percent;

Teamwork

	Before	After
Sales	$29,700,000	$30,296,970
Cost of Goods Sold	21,600,000	21,585,152
Gross Profit	8,100,000	8,711,818
Expenses	7,722,000	7,565,800
Pre Tax Income	$ 378,000	$ 1,146,018
% Change on Pre Tax Income	+ 0%	+ 203%

- Improve inventory turns from five to seven;
- Reduce DSO by five days.

In closing, Scott said, "Opportunity lies in the decisions each of you make every day. Since I can't be involved in all those decisions, it becomes your responsibility to make decisions that will move us toward our goal. I'm confident in your ability to make that happen."

The branch meeting ended on a positive note. What had previously seemed out of reach now seemed achievable. Everyone left the meeting feeling confident they had a simple action plan that would contribute to a turnaround at BD.

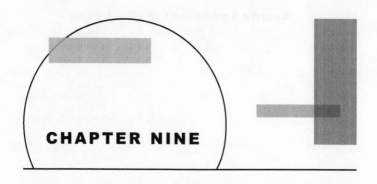

CHAPTER NINE

What happened to Jake during the following weeks was amazing. The more he focused on protecting his sell price, the better he got at it. He won business with less price discounting and managed to increase margins on certain items and products that were less price-sensitive. Sure, he got pushback from customers and it didn't work all the time, but it worked more often than he had anticipated.

"Steve, let's go to Hamptons after work and invite Sue Ho along," Jake suggested one afternoon, feeling energized by his recent successes.

Steve was perplexed. "Hamptons sounds good, but why invite Sue?"

"Because she generates more margin dollars than any other rep. I want to find out how she does it."

Steve reluctantly agreed to invite her.

At 4:30 PM, the three colleagues met at Hamptons. After some small talk, Jake asked Sue what she thought of the management change.

"I liked Kirk," Sue began. "His intentions were good, but Scott really knows how to run a business. He understands the profit drivers and profit leaks in this business far better than Kirk did. More importantly, he knows how to draw the best out of people and let them discover how to improve their part of the business versus just telling them what to do. What do you guys think?"

"I feel like I'm on the right track," Jake replied. "I know I've made some progress in the last few months. It may not be enough to show up on the financials, but I'm definitely moving in the right direction."

"That's great. What about you, Steve?"

"I agree," Steve said. "Scott's been great for the business and we'll make progress, but I don't think it'll be easy. Most reps still take low-margin business in order to make the sale so they get closer to quota and still earn some commission. Their primary concern is 'what's in it for me?' The other red flag for me is that it's easy to announce a 1 percent price increase, but customers may not go along with it."

"You're probably right about the reps accepting low-margin business," Sue interjected, "but don't they realize that the more value they create, the more valuable they become—not only to BD but potentially to future employers as well? I've had a couple of job offers from competitors in the past year."

Steve was shocked. "You've had a couple of offers!" he exclaimed.

"Yes, and I came very close to accepting them because I would have made more money."

"Why didn't you accept?"

"Because I haven't been here that long and I don't want to be seen as a person who job- hops from one company to another. I wanted to give BD a little more time and make sure that when I do move internally or externally, it's a promotion and not a lateral move."

"Wow! I had no idea you had those offers," Steve said.

"Those opportunities are out there. My father always told me that if you are good at what you do, you will always be in demand, regardless of the economy. That's why I work hard to generate more profit for BD. It took awhile, but ultimately I got recognized for my efforts."

Anxious to learn more, Steve pressed on. "I'm curious to find out how you've been more successful than anyone else at improving margins and generating profit."

"I think it's the way I operate," Sue explained. "For example, I work hard at building relationships with customers because when they want to deal with you, price becomes a little less important. I work hard at being reliable—getting orders out quickly, following up to make sure the order arrives on time, etc. Let's face it, reliability has some value in the eyes of customers. I work hard at communicating how BD's solutions add economic and operational value to their business. I also think in smaller price increments. Why leave money on the table? Furthermore, I always try to sell higher-margin products first. Sometimes higher margin products are better for the customer and us. Competing on price is my last option and if I discount price, I always try to get new business from that customer.

"In summary, I try not to give my customers a reason to shop around. These ideas don't work all the time, but they work more often than you'd expect. In the long run, if you do these things often enough you'll raise margins like I have. "

"What if the customer still asks for a price concession?"

"Unless it's an unusual circumstance, I'm prepared to walk away from the business. My goal is to generate more profit, not to price BD out of business. There are always customers out there who buy only on price, and that's fine. I'll focus on more profitable customers and let someone else have the low-margin business. As you know we don't have a low enough cost structure to play the low margin volume game."

Time flew by and before Jake knew it, they were all on their way home. Jake had been unaware Sue had received job offers and that she was so serious about her profession and building a business. Jake and Steve had both gained new respect for Sue and made a point of remembering her tips.

That same evening, the Millers were scheduled to drop by Jake's house for coffee. Jake normally preferred to socialize with friends on weekends only, but he was anxious to continue his discussion on personal finance with Ben.

"They're late. It's only a little after eight o'clock, but I'm tired," Jess complained, yawning.

"Me, too. You know you're getting old when eight o'clock seems late," Jake quipped.

The Millers arrived twenty minutes later. Fortunately for Jake, he and Ben got into their own discussion early. As it turned out, Ben had been looking forward to discussing the 1 percent difference. Jake brought Ben up to speed on the events of their sales meetings and the small successes he had enjoyed over the past few weeks. Ben listened attentively and asked insightful questions. He recognized a good idea when he saw it. Jake got the impression Ben was planning to run the same exercise with his own employees.

After playing the good host and talking about what his guest was interested in, Jake finally shifted the conversation to personal finance. "Last time you were over Ben you mentioned that people need to change their approach to how they manage money. We talked about the power of compound interest and 'time in the market' versus 'timing the market.' In what other ways do people need to change?"

"That's easy, Jake," Ben replied. "The other two principles I live by are 'spend/invest decisions' and 'pay yourself first'."

"What do you mean by 'spend/invest decisions'?" Jake asked.

Taking a sip of his coffee, Ben explained, "People generally base their purchasing decisions on what they can pay for in cash, put on their credit card, finance or lease. When someone decides to purchase an item—whether it's a new computer or a car—that person has also decided not to save or invest that money. People seldom look at the real cost or what we refer to in business as the 'opportunity cost' of those decisions."

"But what if you need a new computer or new car?"

"If you need it, then go ahead and buy it," Ben advised. "However, don't confuse *needs* with *wants*.

Most people don't *need* a new car; they *want* a new car. You could probably convince me that you need a TV so you can sit back and relax, but you could never convince me that you need the latest big-screen TV. I'm not against buying things you want; just don't confuse *needs* with *wants*. People work hard and should enjoy the fruits of their labor. The problem is that most people spend more than they can afford and don't consider the impact on savings.

"For example, let's assume you need to replace your car and you're one of the very few people who decided not to lease and actually saved $20,000 for this purchase. You're considering either a late model car for $20,000 or an older car for $10,000. Let's also assume that both cars depreciate by 50% over the next three years. My question to you is: how much further ahead are you financially if you buy the $10,000 car at the end of three years?"

"Well, I've saved $10,000 on the initial purchase price with the older car," Jake replied, "but it's also worth $5,000 less at the end of three years, so the difference is really only $5,000."

"Okay, I can buy that logic, but what about the time value of that money? What if you invested the $10,000 initial difference at 10%? How much would it be worth thirty years later?"

"I have no idea."

"I happen to know that it would grow to over $174,000. In other words, you could have a newer car for the foreseeable future, or you could have $174,000 more at retirement."

"Wow!" Jake exclaimed. "I never thought about it that way before."

"That's because you looked only at the spend side of the spend/invest decision," Ben informed him.

"What about extra maintenance costs for an older car, reliability issues and that sooner or later this car will need to be replaced?"

"It would be logical to allow for some extra maintenance. You may even want to reduce the interest rate, although over the long term the stock market has delivered over 10 percent per year. I encourage people to use the variables they think are accurate. In the end, you'll be much further ahead financially if you spend a little less and invest the difference. It doesn't matter if it's $10 less at dinner or $10,000 less on a car—you'll still be further ahead.

"To look at it another way," Ben continued, "you could create a personal income statement. Your income becomes the revenue. Subtract your expenses to determine your savings, and then make 1 percent changes to revenue and expenses and see what happens to savings. Finally, determine how much those savings are worth at retirement. You'll be amazed at the outcome."

"I just might try doing that exercise," Jake said. "What about the 'pay yourself first' principle? Does this mean developing a budget to make sure you save?"

"Not exactly," Ben explained, taking another sip of his coffee. "I'm not a fan of budgets because they don't work for most people. Budgeting is like dieting—you enjoy short-term success but in the end it's no fun and you revert to old habits. I recommend you have money—ideally, 10 percent—automatically withdrawn from your account right after you deposit your payroll check. Put this money in an account you won't touch, and then do whatever you want with the remaining 90 percent. There is no budget or records to maintain."

"But if I'm having a hard time saving now, how will I survive on 10 percent less?"

"It might be a bit of a hardship at first," Ben admitted, "but you'll adapt. I'll wager that you survived just fine a couple years ago when you made 10 percent less. After all, you're still here. The problem is that people increase their standard of living when their pay increases, so they never save. You could give most people a 20 percent raise and they still couldn't save money. If you discover it's an absolute hardship to save 10 percent, then try 5 percent, but don't forget the power of compound interest over time. Remember, if you save just two hundred dollars per month from age twenty to sixty-five and earn 10 percent interest, you'll end up with about two million dollars."

After the Millers left at ten o'clock, Jess and Jake stayed up and talked for another hour.

"You know, Jess, I think the ideas Scott and Ben shared are simple, practical and powerful. I wish someone had shared them with me fifteen years ago."

"Didn't you learn those things at college?"

"No, I don't know why they didn't focus on principles like these, especially in the business program I was in. Schools should teach money management principles to everyone because ultimately we all manage and spend money. The 1 percent difference principles apply to anyone who makes business decisions. You may be a retail store owner, an architect, a veterinarian, a manager or a sales rep like me—the universality of these principles apply to everyone in business."

"Well, at least you're learning them earlier in life as opposed to later," Jess noted. "You still have thirty years of work to apply them."

"Did you have to phrase it that way?" Jake said, groaning. "Thirty years sounds like an eternity."

After working through all the agenda items at the July sales meeting, it was time to review the monthly numbers.

Scott put up a slide with a table showing comparative results for the period. "The good news is that margins were up .5 percent last month," he said. "Congratulations! That's tremendous progress in such a short period of time."

Everyone in the room heaved a sigh of relief. They had finally made progress on their margin goal. Sales were still relatively flat, but the higher margins resulted in an almost 50 percent improvement in profitability for the period. Scott drilled down to another level that showed the increase in sales for the XL line.

After further review and discussion about margins, Scott stated, "Before we finish, I have three announcements to make. Effective August 1, the Sales Compensation Program will be modified slightly so you will earn more on high-margin orders and less on low-margin orders. This is a corporate program and the details have yet to be finalized, but I think it's safe to assume that those of you who generate more margin dollars will see an increase in pay and those who discount to get volume may experience a decrease in pay. I want to reiterate that this is only a change to the existing program, not an entirely new program. Over the next two weeks, I'll be arranging meetings with all of you to review your results and the anticipated impact on pay."

The announcement received mixed reactions. Reps like Sue, who generated more margin dollars, were delighted while reps like Donna, who were known as "price-cutters," were disappointed. There were more questions than answers—not everyone was satisfied. Scott had alerted them to the upcoming changes, but the reps wanted more details.

"My second announcement is that, effective today, I'm implementing a sales contest that rewards margin dollars and margin-dollar improvement. This is how it will work: the two reps who generate the most margin dollars will each receive a trip for two to a yet-to-be-determined destination. In addition, the two reps who show the biggest improvement in margin contribution on a percentage basis from the previous six months will also receive a trip for two to a destination yet to be determined. The winners for the January-to-June period will be announced in August. The winners of the July-to-December period will be announced in February next year."

Applause erupted and the energy in the room escalated. Sales reps love contests!

"And finally," Scott announced, "if anyone feels like having a free beer, I'm buying! I'll be at Hampton's in fifteen minutes if anyone wants to join me."

The reps cheered. It was an offer they couldn't refuse!

Scott was a team-builder; he gave everyone an equal chance and treated everybody with respect. Ultimately, though, people would have to perform if they wanted to be on his team . . . and *everybody* wanted to be on Scott's team.

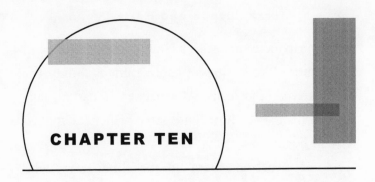

CHAPTER TEN

What most people don't know about the Pacific Northwest is that it's often very dry and hot in the summer. August 10 was one such day. That evening, Jess hosted a cookout for a few friends and neighbors.

Their guests arrived at about 7:00 PM. The men gathered around the barbeque outside while the women chatted in the kitchen. After a delicious meal out on the deck, everyone relaxed and enjoyed the atmosphere and casual conversation. As the evening wore on, the men remained outside, talking about subjects near and dear to their hearts—sports, cars, vacation and business.

Jake and Jess had an eclectic group of friends over that evening. Jerry was a veterinarian; Bob owned a renovation business that employed a handful of employees; Jack was a supervisor at a small manufacturing company, and Terry ran the local YMCA. Jake told them about Scott—how he'd begun to turn BD around and how a large part of it was getting everyone to focus on decisions they made everyday and think more like business people, understanding the profit drivers and leaks. After some discussion, Jake showed his friends how these same principles applied to their businesses.

Some situations were unique—like Terry, who ran the YMCA. His goal wasn't to maximize profit but rather to cover costs and generate a small surplus. Although technically it was an association, in Jake's mind it was just a different type of business. In fact, it was a larger business than most people realized and needed to operate like a business. It had revenue and expenses and, if run efficiently, would grow and prosper and more people would benefit from it by becoming members. If run poorly, the facilities and programs would deteriorate and lose their appeal. If they didn't generate an adequate surplus to reinvest into the facility, they would eventually become less competitive and lose some of their membership base. In Jake's view, it didn't matter if it was a non-profit service business, a manufacturing plant or a veterinarian hospital—it was still a business, and the principles applied in one way or another.

As the conversation progressed, a couple of the men became more engaged; they could see the opportunity and potential. Jerry, the veterinarian, demonstrated a surprisingly high level of interest. Initially, Jack, the supervisor at a small manufacturing plant, didn't see much of a connection, but when they explored scenarios like small increases in throughput and reducing waste by 1 percent, the light went on for him, too.

The sales reps attended the August sales meeting, eager to see the results of the January-to-June sales contest. After working through the agenda, Scott put up a slide showing the contest winners. Sue Ho and Steve Butler won for generating the most margin dollars while Jake and Donna received the prize for achieving the greatest percentage improvement in generating margin dollars.

Although Jake was thrilled to win, not all was well. Earlier that day, he had lost a $20,000 account based on price.

He broke the news to Scott the next day. "I wanted to thank you for the award and the trip yesterday, but I'm afraid all is not well with my results," Jake told Scott glumly.

Scott was unfazed. "Oh? What's the problem?"

"I lost a $20,000 account yesterday in an effort to protect price."

Jake knew Scott didn't like to lose, so he was surprised when Scott appeared to take the news so well. After asking Jake a few questions, Scott opened his desk drawer and pulled out a business card-sized piece of paper with tables on the front and back. He showed Jake the table on the front, indicating how much additional volume was needed to generate the same gross margin dollars when price was cut at different margin levels. Jake had seen these numbers before, but it was a good reminder of how unprofitable it could be to reduce price. Then Scott turned the card over to the table showing how much volume could be lost at different margin levels by a price increase before it negatively affected gross profit dollars. After calculating how much volume Jake had lost in raising his overall margins by 2 percent, they discovered that BD was still much better off financially. Jake was also better off under the new sales compensation program. At that point, Jake realized why Scott wasn't overly concerned—it wasn't much of a loss after all.

The discussion moved on to the Sunrise Grocery account. Several months earlier, Jake had reduced their price, only to discover that what he had thought was a great deal for BD was actually a money-loser. Now it was time to review the account again, and Jake was uncertain as to how he should approach it.

"What does Sunrise want to accomplish? What need are they trying to address?" Scott asked.

"Definitely reducing costs," replied Jake.

"Why do they want to do that?"

Jake hesitated, wondering if this was a trick question or just a dumb question. He assumed it must be a trick question. "Their margins are compressing due to competition, so in order to compete and make money, they need to reduce costs," he answered cautiously.

"So, their primary goal is to make money by reducing costs." Finally, Scott had gotten the picture.

"Yes, that's it."

"So why don't you focus on helping them make more money through margin decisions, product mix changes etc. rather than reducing the cost of the product we supply? You know what happens to our bottom line when we reduce price."

"How do I do that?"

"I'd like you to think about some of the income statement exercises we did. Using the same methodology with the Sunrise financials might lead you to another solution. Let me know if you need more help."

Jake had walked into Scott's office looking for a solution and was walking out with more questions. It would have been a lot easier if Scott had just told him what to do, but that wasn't his style. He would have to figure it out himself.

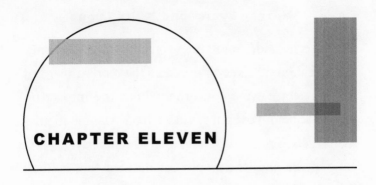

CHAPTER ELEVEN

By the time early October rolled around, it was time for another branch meeting. This one would be short since Scott just wanted to update the branch personnel on their progress over the past few months. After welcoming everyone, he showed a comparative income statement for the first nine months of the year versus the same period last year. Top line sales had increased by 2%, margins had improved by .5% percent, and sales of high margin products, although still below plan, were trending higher. Expenses were down 1.3%. Inventory turns had not improved, but various purchasing initiatives had reduced COGS by .3%. Factoring in all the improvements, overall profitability was up over 125%. It had been a very successful nine months—with all the gain occurring in the past six months!

When Scott proposed they spend $100,000 on office renovations—something employees had wanted for years—he was met with resistance. Surprised by their response, he said, "Sometimes you have to spend money to make money." Everyone wanted the renovations, but several people were concerned about the impact on profitability and overall results. No one wanted to miss the targets, since that would affect bonus pay at year-end. In the end, the employees decided that a small team would develop an improvement plan to be phased in over time.

The biggest surprise came when Scott announced that Sue Ho would assume sales management responsibilities for the branch. She would continue to work her larger accounts and pass her remaining accounts to the other reps. Sue finally got the promotion she was seeking. While Jake was disappointed that he didn't get the job, he realized Sue had begun preparing for it years ago. In the end, he came to grips with the fact that most job offers go to the people who are most skilled and best prepared. Although his results were good, his track record was nothing like Sue's.

Scott ended the meeting by telling a story.

"In the late 1800s and early 1900s, Russell Conwell delivered a famous speech called *Acres of Diamonds* about six thousand times. That's right, one speech delivered six thousand times! Several million people heard Conwell's speech, which was inspired by the legend of a prosperous Persian farmer who deserted his fruitful lands to search for immense wealth. As the legend goes, the farmer died without ever finding the elusive diamond fields. It was only after his death that a huge diamond deposit was found on his own land. The key message Russell learned was this: *Your diamonds are not in faraway mountains or distant seas; they are in your own backyard, if you will only look for them.*

"Virtually every business and employee is searching for "acres of diamonds," their competitive edge," Scott continued, paraphrasing the story. "Unfortunately, when you find that edge, it's just a matter of time before you lose it. It may last only a couple of weeks, or, if you're lucky, a year or two. Companies typically invest significant amounts of time and money to achieve these competitive advantages. Sometimes these initiatives pay off, but often they don't. The good news is that you don't have to invest significant amounts of time and resources to increase profitability. Those 'acres of diamonds' are literally right in your own backyard—in the form of all those decisions you make every day. You just need to start picking them up . . . and you've already done a great job of getting started!

"We've made significant headway over the past six months, but that doesn't mean we're without challenges. New business models and changing customer expectations will force us to change again and again. The cost pressures our customers face will not disappear. We need to continue with 1 percent thinking and at the same time become more competitive through the products and services we offer. Together, we'll make this happen!"

Inspired by Scott's story and encouraged by the results, the reps left the October meeting with renewed hope. BD had clearly started down the path to success!

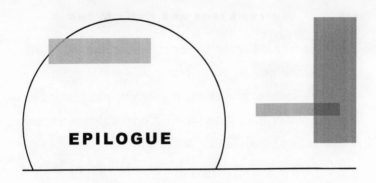

EPILOGUE

Soon the year came to a close. As usual, the last quarter was soft because of the holidays. Overall, the Seattle branch finished much better than was originally forecast. Ten months later, when the branch's performance improved significantly again, Head Office asked Scott to take over management of another BD branch that was struggling. Scott had demonstrated his value to the organization as a turnaround artist. The Seattle branch employees missed Scott, but his ideas remained solidly ingrained in their thinking and actions.

It had been a year of learning for Jake and the other team members. Jake considered himself very fortunate to have worked for Scott. With Scott's help, he discovered how his decisions affected profitability, which enabled him to become a better businessperson. He created value for BD and, thus, became a more valuable employee—a fact that was reflected in his increased earnings and responsibilities.

With some of his extra commission, Jake purchased that big-screen TV for his family room he always wanted and was financially much better off.

BD's main competitor in Seattle offered Jake a job, but like Sue Ho, he refused, wanting to give BD more time. Employee morale was great, and new opportunities at BD were emerging. BD had become much more competitive and was experiencing success. It was now a fun place to work; no one wanted to leave. In fact, BD's Seattle branch was the employer of choice in the local distribution market. After all, everybody wants to work for a winner!

ABOUT THE AUTHORS

Murray and Kelly Lyons specialize in helping organizations improve profitability by focusing on the decisions employees make everyday. Recognizing that most employees do not have a financial background and are often disinterested or intimidated by numbers they set out to develop a highly engaging and experiential way to help employees discover the difference they can make to profitability. The result was a one-day workshop called PROFIT ADVENTURE™. Initially PROFIT ADVENTURE™ was positioned as an add-on service to their consulting and M&A work but quickly became a mainstay of their business. Since 2001 thousands of employees have participated in the workshop. In addition to facilitating they regularly speak at conferences, tradeshows and retreats. They have worked with many organizations ranging in size from small family run companies to large multinational corporations where they have achieved a mark improvement in financial performance.

For more information on how you can help improve financial performance for your employees visit www.profitadventure.com, www.klyons.com or call 1 800 541-9672.

Made in the USA
Lexington, KY
30 December 2010